COUPLES THERAPY WORKBOOK

Restoring Lasting Trust and Deepening Lifelong Intimacy. Proven Strategies, Exercises and EFT Skills for Elevating Communication and Cultivating a Flourishing Relationship.

3 EXTRA BONUSES INCLUDED

🎁 **Interactive Couples Journal**

🎁 **Three Secrets to Reignite Passion in half-a-minute**

🎁 **Ten Power-Packed Hacks for Fast-Track Betrayal Healing**

Esther Collins

Extra Bonus

Inside the book

Scroll to the end and scan the QR Code

Table of Contents

INTRODUCTION

Relationships, with their inherent nature and intricate complexities, are akin to beautifully woven tapestries, comprised of emotions, experiences, and memories. Each relationship, distinct in its essence, often encounters common challenges such as misunderstandings, trust issues, communication barriers, and emotional disconnections. This workbook is designed to be comprehensive, addressing universal relationship challenges.

At the heart of relationships is a pivotal moment when couples find themselves at a crossroads, seeking guidance and tools to reignite their passion and strengthen their bond. This is where the true magic of relationship workbooks comes into play. These are not mere collections of pages; they are transformative tools that accompany couples on a journey of self-discovery and mutual understanding.

This workbook offers a pathway guiding couples through the labyrinthine depths of their emotions, beliefs, and behaviors. It serves as a roadmap, leading couples through the multifaceted aspects of their relationship – from unraveling communication patterns to rebuilding trust. Consider the story of Jamie and Alex, for example. Facing challenges, they turned to this workbook, which introduced them to practical exercises designed to address their unique issues, facilitating conversations and helping rebuild trust.

Unlike traditional books, workbooks are interactive, encouraging couples to actively participate, reflect, and engage fully with the material. This active involvement ensures that the lessons have a personal impact, regardless of someone's sexual orientation or gender identity.

Workbooks also create a space for dialogue. With guided exercises and prompts, couples can navigate topics with the support of a structured format. According to a study published in the Journal of Relationship Research, structured communication exercises can reduce conflicts in relationships by up to 67%.

Many workbooks incorporate techniques such as Emotionally Focused Therapy (EFT) and the Gottman Method, which have shown remarkable success in strengthening relationships across various contexts.

Furthermore, not all couples can easily access regular therapy sessions. Workbooks offer an accessible alternative, empowering couples to nurture their relationship at their own pace and in their own space.

As Dr. John Gottman once said, "Every positive action you take in your relationship is, like foreplay." As you progress through this workbook, remember that every activity, discussion, and moment of self-reflection brings you closer to a more intimate connection with your partner. As you explore the following chapters, filled with theories, real-life situations, exercises, and resources designed for couples like yourselves, approach them with an open heart and mind. Some of the exercises might challenge your beliefs and push you out of your comfort zone, but it's often through these moments of discomfort that we experience growth. So, let's embark on this journey together, embracing love in all its diverse manifestations.

HOW THIS GUIDEBOOK CAN TRANSFORM YOUR RELATIONSHIP

Like tending to a garden, relationships require consistent care, attention, and nurturing to thrive. Over time, various external factors such as work, family, health, and societal expectations can create challenges within even the most solid partnerships. If these challenges are left unaddressed, they can grow into misunderstandings, emotional distance, or even resentment. However, similar to how a gardener tends to their plants with care and dedication, couples have the ability to mend these cracks and ensure that their relationship remains vibrant and strong.

That's where this transformative guidebook comes in. Let me explain how it can serve as a catalyst for change within your relationship:

1. Guiding You on the Path of Self Discovery: Many relationship difficulties stem from a lack of self-awareness. This guidebook provides exercises that encourage introspection, helping you gain an understanding of your own emotions, triggers, and behaviors. By becoming more aware of yourself as an individual within the partnership dynamic, you create an opportunity for understanding between you and your partner. For instance, by recognizing your sources of stress or pressure outside the relationship context itself, you can differentiate between external factors impacting your dynamics versus genuine issues within your connection—thus avoiding unnecessary conflicts.

2. Strengthening Communication Bridges: Effective communication is the foundation of any thriving relationship. This workbook presents methods and exercises inspired by renowned approaches like the Gottman Method, promoting open, sincere, and understanding communication. By practicing these techniques, you and your partner can establish a connection where both feel heard and appreciated.

3. Rediscovering Emotional Intimacy: As time passes, the busyness of life can sometimes create a distance between couples. This workbook encourages partners to reconnect on an emotional level through various activities. Whether it involves revisiting memories, envisioning the future together, or simply understanding each other's love languages, these exercises reignite the emotional flame and remind couples of the love that binds them.

4. Tools for Resolving Conflicts: Disagreements are natural in any relationship. However, how couples handle these disagreements can either strengthen or weaken their bond. Drawing from principles found in Emotionally Focused Therapy (EFT), this workbook provides tools and strategies to navigate conflicts in a constructive manner. Instead of getting caught up in blaming one another, couples learn to approach disagreements with empathy while seeking solutions that honor both partners.

5. Resources at Your Disposal: Besides the exercises and techniques mentioned earlier, this workbook introduces readers to a range of resources such as insightful books, podcasts, as well as helpful apps and websites. These selected resources provide valuable support and knowledge to help couples nurture their relationship effectively.

6. A Plan for Steady Relationship Progress: Consistency plays a vital role in the growth of a relationship. The provided Weekly Therapy Plan offers couples an approach to ensure they set aside regular time for their relationship. By putting in effort week after week, the bond between partners becomes stronger and more resilient.

7. An Adventure of Fun and Personal Development: Relationships are not just about addressing challenges; they also involve creating enjoyable moments and treasured memories. This workbook ensures that the journey includes both introspection and lighthearted fun activities. It is designed to help couples grow while also enjoying time together.

In the words of Dr. Sue Johnson, a prominent figure in Emotionally Focused Therapy, "Love has an incredible ability to heal the profound wounds that life sometimes inflicts upon us." This workbook, with its combination of theory, exercises, and additional resources, serves as evidence of this belief. By dedicating time and effort, couples can tap into the power of love and transform their relationship into a source of happiness, support, and unwavering companionship.

Dear Reader

I genuinely hope that this book has offered you insights and advice on how to cultivate a relationship.

As an independent author your input is incredibly valuable to me.

Your opinion holds importance so I kindly request you to consider writing an honest review. By following this link, it will directly take you to the Amazon reviewing page:

https://www.amazon.com/review/create-review/?asin=**B0CJSYZW57**

Will only take around 30 seconds of your time.

Thank you sincerely for your support.

Warmest regards,

Esther Collins

PART I: UNDERSTANDING THE DYNAMICS OF RELATIONSHIPS

The Importance of Trust

Trust is often likened to the foundation of a house. Just as a strong base is essential for a house to withstand pressures, trust plays a pivotal role in relationships, helping them thrive even in challenging times. What exactly does trust mean, and why is it so essential within relationships? To understand this, we need to explore the aspects behind trust.

The Psychology Behind Trust

At its core, trust involves believing in the reliability, truthfulness, or abilities of someone or something. It encompasses both rational aspects, as we expose our vulnerabilities while having faith that others will not exploit them. From a psychological standpoint, trust is deeply influenced by our earliest experiences. As infants, when we cried, someone was there to address our needs, be it hunger, comfort, or simply seeking interaction. These consistent responses from caregivers instilled in us a fundamental sense of trust in the world and its inhabitants.

As we grow older, our interactions and experiences either reinforce or challenge this foundational trust. Past betrayals, disappointments, or traumas can shake our belief in others and even ourselves, making it difficult to place our faith in people again. Conversely, positive experiences where our trust is honored and reciprocated strengthen our belief in the goodness of individuals.

Trust plays a significant role in romantic relationships, going beyond simply believing that your partner won't cheat or lie. It encompasses the confidence that they will be there for you when needed, respect your feelings and opinions, and prioritize the well-being of the relationship.

Various psychological theories underscore the significance of trust. For instance, John Bowlby's Attachment Theory highlights how attachments formed in childhood influence our adult relationships. These attachments, built on trust and consistent caregiving, shape our ability to trust easily and maintain a view of ourselves and our partners.

Similarly, Dr. John Gottman identifies trust as a crucial element for relationship success. According to his research, trust is fostered through everyday moments when partners consistently choose each other above all else. However, if they repeatedly turn away from or act against each other, trust slowly diminishes.

Nurturing trust requires effort. It involves communication, respecting each other's boundaries while thoroughly understanding them, and consistently upholding those boundaries. It also means being transparent, even during uncomfortable situations.

When trust is shattered, it's about accepting responsibility, making things right, and working together to mend the bond. As relationship expert Esther Perel emphasizes trust: "Trust is about being dependable and reliable. It also involves feeling emotionally secure and protected from harm."

Within the pages of this workbook, we will delve into tools, exercises, and insights to comprehend, construct, and nurture trust. Because with trust as the cornerstone, relationships can withstand any tempest and emerge even stronger.

Real-Life Example: Overcoming Betrayal
Allow me to introduce you to Sarah and Alex, a couple in their thirties who had been together for over ten years. Their love story, admired by many, began as high school sweethearts and evolved smoothly into adulthood. They shared dreams, built a home, and were preparing for parenthood. However, like any real-life narrative, their story was not without its trials.

One evening, Sarah discovered messages on Alex's phone revealing an ongoing affair with a coworker. The discovery devastated her. The trust they had painstakingly built over the years crumbled in an instant. Sarah experienced a whirlwind of emotions: anger at the betrayal, sadness as her world seemed to collapse, and confusion in trying to make sense of it all.

Alex, overwhelmed with guilt and remorse, struggled in the initial aftermath. Their conversations were filled with tears, accusations, and despair. Sarah grappled with questions like "How could he do this to me?" and "Was our entire relationship based on lies?" Alex attempted to explain his actions, attributing them to his own insecurities and the allure of forbidden desires, but no explanations could repair the broken trust.

At a crossroads, they had to decide: should they end their relationship or seek assistance in rebuilding it? Despite everything, thcy still loved each other and chose to give their relationship another chance, turning to couples therapy in hopes of finding ways to heal and move forward together.

In therapy sessions, they learned that trust encompasses more than fidelity; it also includes emotional support, understanding, and open communication. Their therapist, Dr. Martinez, used principles from the Gottman Method and Emotionally Focused Therapy (EFT) to guide them towards healing.

One exercise, "Understanding the Betrayal," encouraged them to explore the emotions and circumstances surrounding the affair. Alex opened up about feeling neglected as Sarah's career flourished, leading to feelings of inadequacy. Sarah shared her feelings of being overwhelmed by work and missing the emotional bond they once had. They also took time to reflect on their relationship history and recognized patterns that had contributed to their growing emotional distance. Dr. Martinez introduced them to the concept of "turning towards" each other during times of stress rather than seeking solace elsewhere.

As they invested effort, engaged in open communication, and participated in guided exercises, the couple gradually began to reestablish trust. They set boundaries, implemented regular check-ins, and most importantly, learned how to openly express their emotions and needs.

Dr. Martinez suggested a resource for them, "Hold Me Tight" by Dr. Sue Johnson, a book that delves into attachment and connection dynamics within relationships. Sarah and Alex found this book enlightening as it provided them with an understanding of their own relationship dynamics. Additionally, they explored apps designed specifically to enhance communication and intimacy among couples.

Two years later, Sarah and Alex not only overcame the betrayal but also succeeded in building an even stronger and more resilient relationship together. They discovered the significance of nurturing trust while recognizing the value of maintaining open lines of communication. Their journey stands as proof that although trust can be fragile, with dedication, empathy, and guidance, it can indeed be rebuilt. Betrayal doesn't need to mark the end; instead, it can serve as a start, an opportunity to redefine and fortify the foundations of a relationship.

Mastering Communication: The Skill of Engaged Listening
In the tapestry of human connections, communication serves as the vital thread binding individuals together. Genuine communication surpasses mere words; it encompasses comprehension, empathy, and establishing a connection. At the heart of this comprehension lies the skill of listening.

Engaged listening involves more than just hearing words; it's about tuning into the emotions, intentions, and unspoken messages beneath those words. It requires being fully present, offering undivided attention, and immersing oneself in the moment. Engaged listening is not about waiting for our turn to speak; rather, it's about striving to understand our partner's perspective.

Consider a scenario: Sarah expresses to her partner Mark that she feels overwhelmed with work and lacks support at home. Instead of instantly providing solutions or dismissing her feelings, Mark could respond by saying, "It seems like you're under significant stress and could benefit from some support. Please tell me more about what's happening." This response demonstrates to Sarah that Mark is sincerely attempting to comprehend her emotions and stands by her side.

Now, how can one nurture the skill of listening?

Be Fully Present: In today's era of distractions, it's important to minimize them when engaging in a conversation with your partner. This means setting aside your phone, turning off the TV, and giving your partner your undivided attention. Avoid interrupting them, as it can make them feel unheard and undervalued. If you're unsure about something your partner said, ask for clarification. Express your understanding by saying things like, "So if I understand correctly, are you saying that...?" This shows active engagement and a genuine effort to understand their perspective.

Demonstrate Empathy: Empathy involves understanding and sharing the emotions of another person. Responses like, "That sounds like a difficult situation," or "I can see why that would make you feel that way," can make your partner feel validated and supported.

Avoid Judging: The goal of listening is to understand rather than pass judgment on your partner's point of view. Even if you disagree with their perspective, it's crucial to respect their feelings and opinions.

Provide Feedback: During the conversation, let your partner know you are actively listening and engaged in what they're saying.

Real-life Case Study: From Misunderstandings to Clarity
Sarah and Diego, happily married for five years, discovered that incorporating active listening into their relationship was transformative. By nodding, maintaining eye contact, and using cues like "I understand" or "Go on," they made each other feel genuinely heard.

A study published in the Journal of Social and Personal Relationships revealed that couples who actively practiced listening reported higher levels of satisfaction in their relationships. It became clear that active listening fosters understanding, resolves conflicts, and strengthens the bond between partners.

However, mastering listening required practice. It was a skill that needed to be honed over time. Sarah and Diego were willing to put in the effort, knowing it would be worth it.

As Carl Rogers once stated, "When someone really hears you without passing judgment on you, without trying to take responsibility for you, without trying to mold you, it feels damn good!" These words resonated deeply with both Sarah and Diego as they embarked on their journey towards mastering communication through listening.

They recognized that active listening stood out as a guiding beacon amidst the complexities of their relationship. By embracing this art form with empathy, respect, and love, Sarah and Diego navigated misunderstandings with clarity, deepening their understanding of one another and fostering a stronger connection.

Their commitment to practicing listening not only improved their communication but also brought them closer together. Through engagement with one another's thoughts and feelings, they found renewed joy in their relationship – a joy built upon empathy-filled conversations where both felt truly seen and understood.

Emotionally Focused Therapy (EFT) and the Role of Emotions in Relationships

Emotions are the life force of relationships, serving as the language through which partners express their deepest desires, fears, and needs. From the exhilaration of falling in love to the heaviness of heartbreak, emotions set the rhythm for every relationship. However, emotions can also be intricate, leading to misunderstandings and conflicts. Emotionally Focused Therapy (EFT), pioneered by Dr. Sue Johnson, is a method of couples therapy that prioritizes establishing and reinforcing secure emotional bonds between partners. EFT is grounded in the belief that humans have a fundamental need for connection, and our most significant emotional experiences arise from our interactions with loved ones.

Emotions as Signals: Emotions, whether joy, anger, sadness, or fear, serve as signals communicating our needs, desires, and boundaries. Recognizing these signals is the first step towards understanding both our own emotional landscape and that of our partners.

Emotional Vulnerability: Behind every defensive posture or argumentative stance lies a hidden, vulnerable emotion. EFT supports couples in uncovering these emotions, whether it's fear of rejection, pain from feeling overlooked, or a yearning to be understood. By bringing these emotions into focus, EFT practices facilitate understanding and connection.

Dealing with Repetitive Arguments and Emotional Triggers: Couples often find themselves in repetitive patterns of arguments fueled by underlying emotional triggers. EFT aims to help couples identify and break free from these cycles by understanding the emotions driving them. For example, withdrawal by one partner can trigger feelings of abandonment in the other, leading to criticism and intensifying the withdrawal. Recognizing this cycle and the emotions behind it can pave the way for healthier interactions.

Establishing a Safe Emotional Environment: To foster an emotional connection, couples must feel secure in expressing their emotions without fear of judgment or rejection. EFT emphasizes creating a safe space where both partners can openly share their deepest feelings, fears, and desires. It is within this environment that true healing and connection can occur.

Strengthening Bonds: EFT goes beyond simply understanding emotions; it focuses on using them as a means of reinforcing the bond between partners. By reaching out to one another during emotional moments, couples can build stronger and more resilient emotional bonds. This process involves truly seeing each other and being seen at a profound emotional level.

According to Dr. Sue Johnson, love is a deeply ingrained mechanism that evolved to ensure the closeness of loved ones. Emotionally Focused Therapy uses this understanding, assisting couples in deciphering the language of emotions. By comprehending the significance of emotions in relationships, couples can transition from feelings of detachment and discord to a state of intimacy and comprehension. In the dance of love, emotions serve as the footsteps, while EFT acts as the skilled choreographer guiding couples towards a harmonious rhythm.

Techniques of EFT and Their Advantages
Emotionally Focused Therapy (EFT) is pivotal for couples navigating relationship challenges. It focuses on the importance of emotions in connections and equips couples with tools to reshape their emotional responses, fostering deeper bonds.

Resolving Negative Cycles: A core step in EFT involves identifying and understanding the patterns or cycles couples find themselves in, often characterized by blame, defensiveness, and withdrawal. Recognizing these cycles as the adversaries, rather than each other, promotes collaboration and understanding.

Advantage: Reduces blame and conflict, encouraging a problem-solving approach.

Exploring Vulnerable Emotions: EFT encourages partners to explore their inner world, seeking out vulnerable feelings beneath defensive reactions. This involves accessing and expressing emotions authentically to effectively communicate needs.

Advantage: Facilitates deeper communication by expressing authentic needs and improving how partners express emotions, thereby strengthening their connection.

Changing the Bond: After identifying their cycles and uncovering underlying feelings, EFT helps couples develop new, positive ways of interacting, responding to each other's vulnerabilities with empathy and understanding.

Advantage: Shifts the relationship from conflict and distance to support and closeness.

Integration: This phase focuses on reinforcing the changes achieved during therapy. Couples reflect on their journey, solidify their new patterns, and plan for a future that maintains their progress.

Advantage: Ensures long-term success and resilience when facing challenges.

Healing Attachment Injuries: EFT acknowledges that certain betrayals or hurts, referred to as "attachment injuries," can severely damage relationships. EFT provides an approach to address these injuries by helping the wounded partner express their pain while allowing the other to show genuine remorse and reassurance.

Advantage: Heals profound wounds, paving the way for trust and intimacy.

Creating a Strong Foundation: Inspired by attachment theory, EFT highlights the importance of partners serving as a supportive presence for each other. This includes offering comfort and security. Through various exercises, couples are guided towards deepening their understanding and responsiveness.

Advantage: Cultivates feelings of reassurance, stability, and overall safety within the partnership.

The Gottman Method; A Comprehensive Exploration of "The Seven Principles for Making Marriage Work"

The Gottman Method, developed by Dr. John Gottman and Dr. Julie Schwartz Gottman, is a well-regarded approach in couples therapy, known for its evidence-based approach and effectiveness. The method is centered around the book "The Seven Principles for Making Marriage Work," which has significantly impacted numerous relationships. This method offers practical and proven strategies for strengthening the bonds of marriage, making it a valuable resource for couples looking to enhance their relationship.

Understanding the Seven Principles

Building a Strong Relationship: A solid foundation for any relationship lies in understanding each other's worlds. Love Maps represent the part of our brain where we store all the information about our partner's life. It involves knowing their dreams, aspirations, fears, and the intricate details that make up their world.

Cultivating Fondness and Admiration: It's important to focus on the qualities of our partner and express genuine appreciation for them. Jake often reminisces about the gestures Ava made in the early days of their relationship that brought a smile to his face. By revisiting and cherishing these memories, they keep the flame alive between them.

Choosing Connection over Disconnection: True connection is fostered in moments. Whether it's a gesture, a warm smile, or engaging in brief conversations, turning towards our partner creates stronger bonds. Take Liam as an example; when he shares highlights from his day with Zoe, her listening and active engagement make him feel truly valued.

Allowing Your Partner's Influence: Successful relationships are built on respect and consideration, where both partners value each other's opinions and allow them to have an impact on decision-making. When Maya and Omar were choosing a vacation destination, they made sure to take into account both of their preferences, showing respect and collaboration.

Resolving Problems Together: Not all relationship issues are impossible to solve. The Gottman Method emphasizes the importance of addressing problems and using effective conflict resolution strategies. Whether it's about managing finances or dividing household chores, couples like Nina and Raj have discovered ways to discuss, compromise, and find solutions.

Overcoming Sticking Points: Certain problems in relationships may persist indefinitely without a resolution. However, understanding the desires and aspirations behind these issues can help couples navigate through them. When Sophie expressed her desire to live closer to her family while Alex had reservations, they delved into their motivations, finding ways to meet their fundamental needs without compromising their relationship.

Building Meaningful Connections: Relationships thrive when partners share goals, values, and dreams – creating a shared narrative for their lives together. For Ella and Leo, this meant building a home filled with love, laughter, and cherished memories – a vision that guided their journey as a couple.

Real-life Case Study; Rediscovering Love in a Stagnant Relationship

"Anna and Ben; From Stagnation to Reconnection"

Anna and Ben had been happily married for 15 years. From an outsider's perspective, their relationship appeared flawless. They had two children, successful careers, and a beautiful home. However, beneath the surface, their marriage had reached a standstill. The passionate couple who was deeply connected now found themselves living more like roommates rather than soulmates. Their conversations were limited to matters regarding the children or mundane daily tasks. The intimacy and profound emotional connection they once shared seemed like a memory.

Anna often found herself reminiscing about the early days of their relationship, the spontaneous dates, the long conversations that stretched into hours, and the undeniable chemistry they shared. Ben, however, immersed himself in his work to divert his attention from the growing void in their relationship. It seemed that they were merely existing together, with the vibrant spark between them now seemingly gone.

During a challenging phase filled with misunderstandings and disagreements, Anna stumbled upon a book called "The Seven Principles for Making Marriage Work" by Dr. John Gottman. Intrigued by the potential of the Gottman Method, she decided to introduce it to Ben, hoping it could provide them with some needed guidance.

As they delved into the principles outlined in the book, Anna and Ben began to recognize patterns that had contributed to the stagnation of their relationship. They realized that over time they had stopped engaging with each other. Those small moments of connection – shared jokes or simple touches – had become rare occurrences. They had neglected nurturing their "Love Maps," losing touch with each other's evolving dreams, aspirations, and fears.

Determined to breathe life into their relationship, the couple made a conscious decision to apply these principles in their daily lives. They started by focusing on enhancing their Love Maps and setting aside time each week to reconnect and catch up on each other's lives. They consciously put in the effort to nurture their affection and respect for each other, frequently expressing gratitude for each other's qualities and actions.

One of the exercises that had an impact on them was learning how to actively listen. They realized that over time they had fallen into the habit of hearing each other without truly listening. By practicing listening, they started understanding and acknowledging each other's emotions, resulting in more meaningful and constructive conversations.

Gradually, Anna and Ben noticed a change in their relationship dynamics. The emotional distance that had grown between them began to fade. They rediscovered the joy of being together, reigniting the spark that initially brought them closer.

Today, Anna and Ben attribute the revitalization of their relationship to the Gottman Method. While they acknowledge that every relationship has its ups and downs, they feel equipped with tools to navigate challenges and maintain a bond. Their story is a testament to the effectiveness of the Gottman Method, highlighting how commitment, understanding, and having the tools can help couples overcome stagnation and rediscover the magic that defines a fulfilling relationship.

PART II: PRACTICAL TOOLS AND ACTIVITIES

Exciting and Enjoyable Activities: Quick Bonding Ideas for Busy Days

In the fast-paced world we live in, couples often find themselves immersed in a whirlwind of responsibilities, deadlines, and commitments. Amidst this chaos, finding quality time for each other can seem challenging. However, the true beauty of relationships lies in those moments – the fleeting glances and quick exchanges that create lasting memories. On days when time is scarce, quick bonding activities can serve as a bridge that connects two hearts. Here's a handpicked selection of engaging activities that require minimal time but offer maximum connection:

Five-Minute Journaling: End your day by spending just five minutes journaling together. Each partner can write down one thing they appreciate about the other. Sharing these notes can be a heartwarming way to start or end a day while reminding each other of the love that binds you.

Two-Minute Compliment: Take turns giving each other a genuine compliment. It could be about a trait, a recent achievement, or even an outfit choice – these words of affirmation have the power to uplift moods and strengthen your bond.

Let's Take a Stroll Down Memory Lane: Whether it's over a morning cup of coffee or an evening snack, why not share a treasured memory from the early days of your relationship? Reminiscing about those moments that brought you closer can reignite the spark even on hectic days.

Create a Playlist: Make a playlist of three songs that remind you of your partner or your relationship. Swap and listen to them during your commute or workout. It's a way to feel connected even when you're physically apart.

The 10-Minute Dance: Just put on your favorite song and have a spontaneous dance session in the living room. It's not about the moves, but rather the laughter and joy that come with it. This impromptu activity can lighten the mood and bring you closer in no time.

Cooking Together: If time is limited, cooking together can still be a bonding activity. Choose a simple recipe like a salad or sandwich and prepare it as a team. The act of creating something together can be incredibly satisfying.

Thoughtful Text Messages: Throughout the day, send each other thoughtful text messages expressing gratitude for something specific. It could be appreciation for completing chores, providing support, or simply being there for each other.

In Relationships, It's Often the Small Things: Take a moment to gaze at the stars together if you have access to a balcony or backyard. This peaceful activity can serve as a reminder of the vastness of the universe and the special bond you share.

Board Games: Enjoy a session of board games like Tic Tac Toe, Hangman, or card games. These games not only provide a break from your usual routine but also bring out the playful side of your relationship.

Discussing Shared Dreams or Goals: Spare a few minutes to discuss and explore shared dreams or goals with your partner. It could be planning a vacation, learning a new skill together, or envisioning future milestones. This conversation will serve as a reminder of your shared journey and the dreams that unite you.

Remember, it's these moments that create lasting memories and strengthen the foundation of love and commitment in your relationship. On busy days, don't forget that bonding doesn't always require hours; sometimes all it takes is just a few minutes of genuine connection.

Exploring the Depths of Your Relationship: Exploring the depths of your relationship is crucial for its growth, much like tending to a garden. While quick bonding activities are great for connection, it's the in-depth explorations that truly nourish the roots and allow your relationship to blossom. Intimate evenings provide the opportunity to dive deep and embark on a journey of self-discovery together. Here are a few curated activities specifically designed for those special evenings when you and your partner are ready to delve within yourselves and strengthen your bond:

In-Depth Exploration Activities for Intimate Evenings
Mapping Our Dreams: Begin by jotting down your dreams and aspirations on separate pieces of paper. Once you're done, combine these dreams and start mapping out how they intersect, complement each other, or perhaps even present challenges. This activity not only promotes understanding but also helps align your future goals.

The "What If" Game: Take turns asking thought-provoking "What if" questions. For example, "What if we had met ten years earlier?" or "What if we decided to live in a different country?" This game can lead to discussions, laughter, and a deeper understanding of each other's perspectives.

Relationship Time Capsule: Gather keepsakes that hold meaning in your relationship, like tickets from a memorable date, photographs, or small notes. As we place each item in a box, let's talk about the memories attached to them. We can seal the box with the intention of opening it years later, giving us a tangible reminder of our journey together.

Thought-Provoking Questions: Create a list of thought-provoking questions that we've never asked each other before. Questions like "What's a fear you've never shared with me?" or "How do you imagine our life in 10 years?" can lead to meaningful conversations.

Expressing Our Love Through Art: Choose a medium such as painting, clay modeling, or even writing to express our love. Let's discuss what inspired us, the challenges we faced during the process, and the joy it brought us.

Book Club for Two: Select books on relationships, such as John Gottman's "The Seven Principles for Making Marriage Work." Read a chapter separately, then come together to discuss it. This not only enhances our understanding of each other but also introduces new tools and techniques to navigate through different aspects of our relationship.

Creating a Slideshow: Make a slideshow filled with photos and videos from various stages of our journey together. It will be like taking a trip down memory lane and cherishing all those moments.

Creating a Vision Board: Gather magazines, printouts, or personal photos to create a vision board that reflects our shared goals and dreams. This activity will help align our aspirations and foster teamwork.

Switching Roles: Have an evening where we role-play as each other. It could be a fun exercise that reveals insights into how we perceive one another and the roles we play in our relationship.

Sensory Exploration: Plan an evening dedicated to exploring our senses. We can try different cuisines, listen to various genres of music, or experiment with aromatic oils. During this experience, let's discuss the emotions and memories these sensations evoke.

Intimate evenings offer us the chance to dive into understanding each other and being understood, as well as exploring new depths of intimacy. These engaging activities are designed to challenge us, provide comfort, and strengthen the connection between us. Remember, it is not about reaching a specific destination; it is the journey itself that holds true significance. It is in those moments of exploration, laughter, tears, and quiet contemplation that relationships find their depth and meaning.

Real Life Example: Rediscovering the Joy of Playfulness

"Liam and Mia: A Journey to Rediscover Laughter"

Liam and Mia, a couple together for seven years, had initially filled their partnership with spontaneous outings, laughter, and a sense of adventure. They often embarked on road trips, enjoyed indoor picnics, or simply danced under the night sky in their backyard. However, as time passed, responsibilities, work pressures, and the monotony of life began to overshadow their playful nature.

Mia, a designer taking on more projects to support their financial goals, and Liam, a schoolteacher buried under stacks of papers to grade, found their conversations, once filled with dreams and laughter, now focused on bills, chores, and schedules.

One evening, after a long day at work, Mia stumbled upon an old photo album from their early dating days. The pictures, displaying their smiles and silly poses, stood in stark contrast to their current reality, deeply affecting Mia. She realized that somewhere along their journey, they had lost the sense of playfulness that once defined their relationship.

Determined to revive that spark, Mia suggested a "Playfulness Pact" to Liam. They committed to dedicating time each week, regardless of their busy schedules, to engage in enjoyable activities, setting a rule to refrain from discussing work, chores, or other responsibilities during this time.

Their initial endeavor was a blindfolded taste-testing game, where Mia prepared dishes and Liam attempted to guess the ingredients. The outcome was amusing, with Liam making wild guesses and Mia teasing him playfully. The following week, they transformed their living room into an improvised campsite, complete with a tent, fairy lights, and indoor s'mores.

As weeks passed, their activities grew more imaginative, including themed movie nights, water balloon fights, and pottery sessions. These playful dates became the highlight of their week, cherished moments where they could let loose, laugh, and reconnect on a deeper level.

The impact of the "Playfulness Pact" was profound. It not only allowed them to rediscover their playful nature but also significantly improved their communication, enabling them to better understand each other's sources of stress and provide effective support when needed.

The laughter and happiness from their outings spilled over into their everyday lives, making challenges easier to handle and strengthening Liam and Mia's connection. Their journey highlights the importance of playfulness in relationships, reminding us that amidst life's busyness, it's crucial to find moments of joy, laughter, and spontaneity. These moments create a lasting bond.

Building Strong Emotional Connections: Unleashing the Power of Vulnerability

In the dynamics of human relationships, vulnerability emerges as a remarkable force that can either strengthen bonds or drive them apart. It's a balance, both risky and rewarding, requiring a leap of faith that can lead to profound intimacy or profound pain. What is it about vulnerability that holds such transformative influence in relationships, particularly romantic ones?

At its core, vulnerability entails revealing ourselves to another person—flaws, scars, dreams, and all. It means shedding the masks we wear and dismantling the walls we erect to expose ourselves—the ones filled with fears, aspirations, setbacks, and ambitions. In a world that often values strength, resilience, and an outward appearance of having it all, being vulnerable may seem counterintuitive or even perilous.

Nevertheless, esteemed researcher and author Brené Brown consistently highlights that vulnerability is not a sign of weakness but serves as the "birthplace" for love, acceptance, belongingness, joy, courage, empathy, creativity." By embracing vulnerability in our lives, we unlock the gateway to connections. Here's why.

Deepening Connection:
When we open up about our deepest truths, fears, and aspirations to our partner, we invite them into the depths of our inner world. This act of sharing creates a bond that goes beyond mere surface-level interactions, nurturing a profound emotional connection. It's akin to handing someone a guide to the chambers of our heart and trusting them to navigate with care.

Building Trust:

Trust is formed in those moments when we consciously choose to be transparent and honest, even if it feels uncomfortable. Each time we reveal our vulnerabilities and witness our partner responding with understanding and empathy, it strengthens the foundation of trust within both them and the relationship.

Encouraging Mutual Vulnerability:
When one partner bravely takes the step towards vulnerability, it often inspires the other to follow suit. This mutual willingness to be open sets in motion a cycle of openness and comprehension where both partners feel truly seen and appreciated.

Facilitating Healing:
Many of us carry wounds from various sources like childhood experiences, past relationships, or personal setbacks. By opening up and sharing these wounds with our partner, we create a haven for understanding, compassion, and healing. It's like allowing rays of sunlight into a room—offering warmth that can help mend old scars.

The benefits of vulnerability extend to growth as well. When we share our fears and insecurities with our partner, it opens up the opportunity for feedback and self-reflection. They can provide a perspective that helps us see things in a new light, fostering personal development.

However, it is important to approach vulnerability with caution. Not every situation or person is deserving of our openness. It's crucial to ensure that the relationship provides a space, free from judgment or criticism before we fully open up. Additionally, vulnerability is not a destination but an ongoing journey that requires continuous effort, reflection, and communication.

In relationships specifically, vulnerability serves as a bridge towards deeper connection and understanding. It acts as the thread that intertwines two souls together, creating a tapestry of shared experiences, emotions, and memories. By embracing vulnerability, couples can unlock an intimacy and connection that withstands the test of time – weathering storms and cherishing moments of shared joy. So let go of your inhibitions, open your heart wide, and embrace the power of vulnerability. Engaging in activities that encourage exploration and connection also plays a significant role in strengthening the bond between partners.

It's not just about comprehending someone's emotions but also about navigating the complex array of feelings that both partners bring into the relationship. Here's a detailed exploration of activities that can foster this deep emotional connection.

Building Strong Emotional Connections: Harnessing the Power of Vulnerability

In the complex world of human relationships, vulnerability stands as a powerful element that can either fortify bonds or lead to their unraveling. It strikes a delicate balance between risk and reward, demanding a leap of faith that can culminate in deep intimacy or, conversely, significant pain. Vulnerability's transformative role in relationships, especially romantic ones, cannot be overstated.

Essentially, vulnerability involves laying bare our true selves to another person, encompassing our flaws, scars, aspirations, and fears. It's about removing the facades we often hide behind and breaking down the walls we've built, allowing our true selves to be seen — complete with our insecurities, hopes, past hurts, and dreams. In a society that frequently glorifies strength and an outward show of perfection, embracing vulnerability might seem counterintuitive or risky.

However, Brené Brown, a renowned researcher and author, consistently emphasizes that vulnerability is not a weakness but rather the cradle of many of life's most fulfilling experiences like love, acceptance, joy, courage, empathy, and creativity. By welcoming vulnerability into our lives, we unlock the door to meaningful connections. The reasons are manifold.

Deepening Connection:
Revealing our innermost thoughts, fears, and aspirations to our partners invites them into our most personal spaces. This sharing fosters a bond that transcends superficial interactions, nurturing a deep emotional connection. It's akin to giving someone a map to the inner workings of our heart and trusting them to navigate it with care and understanding.

Building Trust:

Trust is established when we choose to be transparent and honest, even in discomfort. Each instance where we expose our vulnerabilities and are met with empathy and understanding from our partner reinforces the foundation of trust in the relationship.

Encouraging Mutual Vulnerability:
When one partner steps forward with vulnerability, it often encourages the other to do the same. This reciprocity of openness fosters a cycle of understanding and appreciation, where both partners feel genuinely recognized and valued.

Facilitating Healing:
Most of us carry wounds from various life experiences, such as childhood events, past relationships, or personal setbacks. Sharing these experiences with our partner creates a sanctuary for understanding, compassion, and healing. It's like letting sunlight into a previously darkened room, bringing warmth and healing to past scars.

The benefits of vulnerability also extend to personal growth. When we share our insecurities and fears with our partner, it opens up avenues for feedback and self-reflection, offering new perspectives that foster personal development.

Nevertheless, vulnerability should be approached with discernment. Not every situation or individual warrants our complete openness. It's essential to ensure a relationship space is free of judgment and criticism before fully opening up. Moreover, vulnerability is not a destination but a continuous journey, requiring ongoing effort, reflection, and communication.

In romantic relationships, vulnerability acts as a conduit to deeper connection and understanding. It weaves two individuals together, creating a rich tapestry of shared experiences, emotions, and memories. By embracing vulnerability, couples can unlock a level of intimacy and connection that endures through time, embracing both the challenges and joys of shared life. So, shed your inhibitions, open your heart, and embrace the transformative power of vulnerability. Engaging in activities that promote exploration and connection is also vital in strengthening the bond between partners.

Vulnerability isn't just about understanding someone's emotions but also navigating the complex array of feelings both partners bring into the relationship. Here's an exploration of activities that can foster deep emotional connections.

Recognizing and Dealing with Triggers using EFT and the Gottman Method

Conflicts are a part of any relationship, but the way couples manage these conflicts greatly impacts the health and longevity of their bond. As mentioned in the previous chapters of this book, two effective approaches in couple's therapy, Emotionally Focused Therapy (EFT) and the Gottman Method, provide valuable insights into conflict management, particularly in identifying and addressing triggers.

Understanding Triggers: Many conflicts originate from triggers – events, words, or actions that evoke strong emotional reactions. These triggers often stem from past experiences, unresolved issues, or deep-rooted fears. For example, a casual comment about finances from one partner might trigger feelings of insecurity in the other, stemming from childhood memories of financial instability.

EFT's Approach to Triggers: Developed by Dr. Sue Johnson, EFT emphasizes the connection between partners. Conflicts often arise due to perceived threats to the bond between individuals. When a trigger is activated, it typically indicates an emotional need, leading to feelings of disconnection.

To effectively address triggers using EFT, follow these steps:

1. Recognize the Dance: Emotionally Focused Therapy (EFT) often describes conflict patterns as "dances." The initial step involves recognizing this interaction pattern. For instance, when one partner withdraws, it might trigger the other's pursuit, leading to a recurring pattern of chase and withdrawal. Recognizing this dance is crucial for understanding how your interactions escalate conflicts.

2. Delve Deeper: Instead of focusing solely on the surface-level argument, EFT encourages couples to explore underlying emotions. What deeper fears or needs does the trigger point towards? This step involves moving past the immediate conflict to understand the emotional drivers behind each partner's reactions. It's about identifying feelings like fear, insecurity, or a need for closeness that might be fueling the conflict.

3. Reframe the Narrative: Once you've identified the underlying emotions, it's essential for couples to express these vulnerabilities to each other. The goal is to shift the conflict narrative from a stance of "me against you" to "us against the problem." This reframing fosters a collaborative approach to problem-solving, where both partners see themselves as a team working towards a common goal, rather than adversaries.

In practice, this approach helps couples to not only manage conflicts more effectively but also deepens their emotional connection. It allows for a greater understanding of each other's emotional worlds, fostering empathy and strengthening the bond. By addressing triggers in this empathetic and understanding way, couples can transform potentially divisive moments into opportunities for growth and deeper intimacy.

The Gottman Method's Perspective on Triggers and Activities for Peaceful Conflict Resolution

The Gottman Method on Triggers: Developed by Drs. John and Julie Gottman, this method emphasizes the importance of understanding each other's triggers in managing conflicts. It suggests that while not every conflict needs to be resolved, couples should strive to comprehend each other's triggers and perspectives. This approach helps in navigating conflicts more empathetically, reducing misunderstandings and fostering a deeper connection.

Steps for Dealing with Triggers Using the Gottman Method:

1. **Soft Start-Up:** Begin conversations positively, avoiding criticism or contempt, which can immediately put your partner on the defensive. Express your feelings without assigning blame to your partner.
2. **Responsive Reaction:** How you react to your partner's triggers can either escalate or de-escalate the situation. It's crucial to turn towards your partner by acknowledging and addressing their concerns, rather than turning away.

3. **Understanding Perspectives:** Before trying to find solutions, take time to fully understand each other's viewpoints. This involves active listening and asking open-ended questions to gain insights into each other's perspectives.
4. **Repair Checklist:** The Gottmans developed a list of statements or actions that can help de-escalate situations when triggers are activated. Utilizing this checklist can be beneficial in diffusing tensions and finding resolutions.

Activities for Promoting Peaceful Conflict Resolution

1. **The Safe Haven Exercise:**
   - Purpose: Establish an emotional space where both partners feel valued and understood.
   - Activity: Sit facing each other. Share a situation where you felt vulnerable or hurt, without placing blame. Actively listen, validate the feelings expressed, and provide comfort. Switch roles and repeat.
2. **The Stress-Reducing Conversation:**
   - Goal: Discuss stressors without negatively impacting the relationship.
   - Activity: Set aside 30 minutes. Share a relationship-related source of stress. The listener focuses on understanding and empathy, without offering solutions. Switch roles and repeat.
3. **The Emotional Trigger Map:**
   - Purpose: Identifying and understanding triggers.
   - Activity: Write down situations or behaviors that elicit emotional reactions. Discuss the underlying fears or needs associated with each trigger. Brainstorm ways to support each other.
4. **The Four Horsemen Intervention:**
   - Purpose: Counteracting the four negative behaviors that predict relationship breakdown: criticism, contempt, defensiveness, and stonewalling.
   - Activity: Discuss these behaviors and their remedies. Share instances where you have noticed them in your interactions and commit to employing remedies.
5. **The Attachment Injury Repair Exercise:**
   - Purpose: Addressing wounds that still impact the relationship.

- Activity: Share a hurt or betrayal. The listener acknowledges the pain caused and expresses remorse. Discuss strategies to prevent future injuries.
6. **Dreams Within Conflict Exercise:**
   - Purpose: Understanding the significance behind recurring conflicts.
   - Activity: Identify a recurring conflict. Reflect on underlying dreams or values related to positions in this conflict. Share these dreams and find ways to honor both perspectives.

Incorporating these activities can transform how couples handle disagreements. By dedicating time to these exercises, conflicts can become opportunities for growth, leading to a stronger and more empathetic bond.

A Step-by-Step Guide for Enhancing Relationships

Embarking on a journey towards improving your relationship requires dedication, patience, and a structured approach. Creating a plan for therapy can act as a roadmap guiding couples through various aspects of their relationship, helping them move closer to understanding, intimacy, and harmony. Here's a suggested guide focusing week by week to revitalize and strengthen the bond between you and your partner.

Week 1: Reflecting on Yourself and Setting Goals

Begin your journey by individually reflecting on the state of your relationship. Consider what aspects bring satisfaction and identify areas for improvement. Then, come together for a discussion about your reflections, setting clear, mutually agreed-upon goals for the upcoming weeks.

Main Focus and Goal for This Week:

The focus this week is to establish a strong foundation for future therapy sessions. It involves understanding how your relationship functions, recognizing areas of contentment as well as challenges. The goal is to set objectives for the coming weeks that align with both partners' visions for improving the relationship.

Description of Activities and Duration:

1. **Individual Reflection (30 minutes each):** Each partner takes time alone to jot down thoughts about the current state of the relationship, acknowledging aspects that work well, addressing concerns, and expressing personal desires or hopes for its future.
2. **Discussion Session (1 hour):** Partners come together to share their thoughts and reflections in an environment where each person can express themselves without interruptions, ensuring that both individuals feel heard and understood.
3. **Goal Setting Activity (45 minutes):** Collaboratively, using a template or a blank sheet of paper, partners compile a list of shared goals for their relationship, ranging from enhancing communication to planning dates. The objective is to establish actionable targets for the upcoming weeks.
4. **Creating a Vision Board (1.5 hours):** Partners gather magazines, pictures, and markers to craft a vision board that reflects their dreams and aspirations for the relationship. This visual representation serves as a reminder of their collective aspirations.

Tips for Engaging as Partners:

- **Active Participation:** Both partners should actively engage in each activity. If one partner feels hesitant, it may be helpful to start with tasks before delving into more profound discussions.
- **Establishing a Safe Space:** Ensure the setting promotes open discussions and fosters an atmosphere of trust and respect. This means avoiding distractions like turning off phones and creating an atmosphere with soft lighting and music.
- **Use "I" Statements:** Encourage expressing feelings using phrases like "I feel" or "I believe," without blaming or becoming defensive towards the partner.
- **Patience:** Approach each activity with an open mind and heart. Understand that this is the beginning, and there may be emotions or topics that are difficult to discuss.

Benefits:

- **Clarity:** By the end of the week, both partners will have an understanding of where they stand in their relationship and where they want it to go.
- **Alignment:** The activities ensure that both partners share the same goals for their relationship.
- **Improved Communication:** The joint discussion sessions establish a foundation for communication, teaching partners to listen actively and speak empathetically.
- **Motivation:** Setting shared goals and creating a vision board serves as motivation for the weeks ahead, reminding partners of their commitment to enhancing their relationship.

By dedicating time to reflect on themselves and set goals during the first week, couples are better prepared to navigate challenges and activities in the following weeks. This solid groundwork ensures that the path ahead will be an effort, meaningful, and in harmony with the couple's shared hopes and dreams.

Week 2: Strengthening Connection

In this week, we focus on the art of active listening. We'll engage in exercises that challenge both partners to listen without interruption, ensuring that each person feels genuinely heard and understood. We'll practice reflecting each other's words to validate feelings and thoughts.

Objective and Purpose of Week Two

Our main aim during this week is to deepen the emotional bond between partners. After establishing a foundation with self-reflection and goal setting, it's time to delve further into understanding each other's needs, desires, and vulnerabilities. Our goal for this week is to nurture emotional intimacy where both partners feel acknowledged, listened to, and appreciated in the relationship.

Activities:

1. **Mapping Emotions (Estimated Duration: 30 minutes per person):**

- Individually, partners will map out their frequently experienced emotions over the past month using colors or symbols. This exercise offers insights into their emotional landscape and triggers.

2. **Sharing an Emotional Experience (Estimated Duration: 1 hour):**
   - Partners can choose a movie or read a short story together that evokes strong emotions. Afterwards, they discuss their feelings and reactions, gaining an understanding of how each person processes emotions.

3. **Emotional Vulnerability Exercise (45 minutes):**
   - Find a comfortable place to sit down with your partner. Take turns sharing an experience from the past that had an emotional impact on you. The listener's role is to offer support and understanding without trying to solve the problem or pass judgment.

4. **Gratitude Journaling (20 minutes):**
   - Each day, both partners should write down three things they appreciate about their relationship. At the end of the week, share your journal entries with each other to cultivate gratitude and positivity.

Effective Tips for Engaging as Partners:

- **Embrace Emotional Vulnerability:** This week's activities involve exploring emotions, which may be challenging at times. Approach each activity with openness and a willingness to be vulnerable.
- **Non-judgmental Listening:** When your partner shares their experiences, listen without making judgments or giving unsolicited advice.
- **Regular Check-ins:** Given the emotional nature of this week's activities, it's important for partners to check in with each other regularly, ensuring comfort and willingness to continue.

Benefits:
- **Enhanced Emotional Intimacy:** By the end of the week, partners will have delved into and understood each other's emotions on a deeper level, leading to a stronger emotional connection.
- **Improved Empathy:** Engaging in these activities nurtures empathy, allowing partners to step into each other's worlds and provide support.

- **Positive Reinforcement:** Through gratitude journaling, we ensure that amidst the emotional work, there is also a focus on the positive aspects of our relationship.
- **Trust Building:** Sharing vulnerabilities and emotions in a safe space significantly contributes to building trust, which is crucial for any strong relationship.

In Week 2, we embark on a journey that delves into the heart of our relationship. Our focus lies in deepening our connection so that we can cultivate greater understanding, empathy, and trust – all vital ingredients for a thriving partnership.

Week 3: Emotionally Focused Therapy (EFT) Principles and Emotional Dynamics

This week, we turn our focus to the principles of Emotionally Focused Therapy (EFT), a therapeutic approach emphasizing the importance of emotional connection in enhancing relationships. The main objective for this week is to recognize, comprehend, and navigate through the patterns and triggers within the relationship. By doing so, couples can break free from negative cycles and cultivate a stronger, more secure bond.

Overview of Activities and Durations:

1. **Emotional Cycle Mapping (45 minutes):**
   - Partners work together to map out recurring emotional cycles in their relationship. This exercise helps identify patterns, triggers, and reactions, ultimately leading to understanding how to break negative cycles.
2. **EFT Role Play (1 hour):**
   - Partners engage in role-playing scenarios, taking on each other's reactions during conflicts. This activity promotes empathy and deepens their understanding of one another's emotional responses.
3. **Safe Haven Exercise (40 minutes):**
   - Partners take turns discussing moments when they felt emotionally safe and supported within the relationship. They also explore moments of disconnection with the goal of understanding how to recreate those havens during times of distress.

4. **Emotional Responsiveness Practice (30 minutes daily):**
   - Every day, partners engage in a practice of being emotionally responsive to each other, focusing on the principles of accessibility, responsiveness, and engagement in Emotionally Focused Therapy (EFT). This daily exercise helps reinforce the connection between partners.

Dedicated Tips for Engaging with Your Partner:
   - **Stay Curious:** Approach each activity with curiosity about your partner's emotional world. Avoid making assumptions and instead ask open-ended questions.
   - **Prioritize Safety:** Emotional exploration can often be intense, so it's crucial to ensure that both partners feel safe and respected throughout the process.
   - **Use "I" Statements:** When discussing feelings, express your emotions using "I" statements to avoid placing blame or creating defensiveness.
   - **Seek Understanding Over Solutions:** The primary goal is to gain an understanding of each other's emotions rather than finding immediate solutions.

Benefits:
   - **Deeper Understanding:** By following EFT principles, couples can develop a profound understanding of their emotional dynamics, resulting in increased empathy during interactions.
   - **Breaking Negative Cycles:** Identifying and comprehending recurring emotional patterns allows couples to work towards breaking these cycles and fostering healthier interactions.
   - **Strengthened Emotional Bond:** The activities involved in this practice promote emotional responsiveness and connection, ultimately strengthening the bond between partners.

In Week 3, couples embark on a journey into the core of their emotional dynamics. Applying the principles of Emotionally Focused Therapy (EFT), they gain insights into their emotional patterns, fostering a deeper and more secure bond. This week sets the groundwork for navigating future challenges with understanding, empathy, and connection.

Week 4: Conflict Management with the Gottman Method

In Week 4, we delve into the principles of the Gottman Method, specifically exploring the "Four Horsemen" of relationship apocalypse. Participants learn to identify these communication patterns and practice techniques to counteract them, ultimately fostering a more positive dynamic in their interactions. The focus of this week is dedicated to introducing participants to the research-based Gottman Method. This approach delves into communication patterns that can either strengthen or weaken relationships. Our primary objective is to familiarize participants with the "Four Horsemen" – Criticism, Contempt, Defensiveness, and Stonewalling – which have been identified by Dr. John Gottman as destructive communication behaviors within relationships. The goal is for participants to recognize these patterns, understand their impact on their relationship, and acquire techniques for mitigating them in order to promote healthier communication.

Four Horsemen

Criticism
Dealing with problems through harsh, blaming, or hurtful expressions of judgment or disapproval.
• Focus is on perceived personal flaws rather than changeable behaviors.
• Often met with defensiveness.

"This kitchen is a mess. You're such a slob."

Defensiveness
Deflecting responsibility for your own mistakes and behaviors, or refusing to accept feedback.
• Making excuses for behavior.
• Shifting blame to your partner.

"It isn't my fault I yelled. You were late, not me!"

Contempt
Showing anger, disgust, or hostility toward your partner.
• Using putdowns or insults.
• Acting superior to your partner.
• Using a mocking or sarcastic tone.

Stonewalling
Emotionally withdrawing, shutting down, or going silent during important discussions.
• Often a response to feeling overwhelmed.
• Used to avoid difficult discussions or problems.
• Underlying problems go unresolved.

Antidotes

Gentle Startup
Dealing with problems in a calm and gentle way. The focus is on the problem—not the person.
• Save the discussion for an appropriate time.
• Use warm body language and tone of voice.
• Use "I" statements.

"I feel frustrated when dirty dishes are left in the sink. Could you please do the dishes tonight?"

Take Responsibility
Own up to your behavior without blaming others.
• Avoid taking feedback personally.
• Use feedback as an opportunity to improve.
• Show remorse and apologize.

"I shouldn't have raised my voice. I'm sorry."

Share Fondness & Admiration
Foster a healthy relationship by regularly showing each other respect and appreciation.
• Show affection.
• Recognize your partner's strengths.
• Give compliments.

Use Self-Soothing
Use relaxation techniques to calm down and stay present with your partner.
• Agree to pause the conversation briefly.
• Use deep breathing.
• Use progressive muscle relaxation (PMR

Week 4: Conflict Management with the Gottman Method
Activity Descriptions and Timings:

1. **Identifying the Four Horsemen (40 minutes):**
   - Partners will watch or read scenarios showcasing the Four Horsemen in action. They will then discuss instances where they might have unintentionally used these behaviors in their interactions.
2. **Practicing Antidotes (1 hour):**
   - The Gottman Method offers communication strategies as antidotes to each of the Four Horsemen. Partners will engage in role-playing exercises to practice these antidotes, ensuring they can apply them effectively in real-life situations.
3. **Softened Start-Up Exercise (30 minutes):**
   - Instead of initiating discussions with criticism, partners will practice starting conversations gently, focusing on their feelings and needs without assigning blame.
4. **Recognizing Repair Attempts (45 minutes):**
   - Partners will learn about "repair attempts," efforts made during conflicts to defuse tension. They'll reflect on conflicts and identify moments when either partner made a repair attempt, emphasizing the importance of recognizing and responding positively to these attempts in the future.

Tips for Engaging as Partners:
- **Keep an Open Mind:** Recognizing negative communication patterns can be challenging. Approach the activities with an open mind and a willingness to learn and develop.
- **Make it a Habit:** It's most effective to practice the strategies that counteract negative communication patterns regularly. Commit to integrating them into your interactions.
- **Emphasize the Positive:** While it's important to acknowledge any negative patterns, also take time to appreciate and celebrate the positive communication habits you both possess.

- **Seek Clarity Together:** If you're uncertain about a concept or technique, discuss it with each other. Explore additional resources for better understanding.

Benefits:

- **Enhanced Communication:** By recognizing and addressing the communication patterns known as the Four Horsemen, couples can significantly enhance the overall quality of communication.
- **Reduced Conflict:** With the tools and techniques from the Gottman Method, couples can navigate disagreements in ways leading to a decrease in the intensity and frequency of conflicts.
- **Stronger Bond:** As couples replace negative communication patterns with positive ones, they cultivate a deeper connection that is more resilient over time.
- **Improved Understanding:** The activities foster comprehension of each partner's emotions, needs, and unique communication styles, resulting in more empathetic interactions.

During Week 4 of this program, couples gain tools to identify and counteract some of the most damaging communication patterns commonly found in relationships. Incorporating the principles of the Gottman Method helps create a foundation for more positive interactions, leading to a stronger and more resilient relationship.

Week 5: Ignite the Flame

After laying the foundation in previous weeks, it's time to focus on activities specifically designed to rebuild or strengthen trust. This involves engaging in exercises that require partners to depend on each other and having conversations about past betrayals and the journey towards healing.

Focus and Goal of the Week: This week is dedicated to reigniting the connection that may have diminished over time. Intimacy goes beyond proximity; it encompasses emotional bonding, understanding, and sharing aspirations. The aim is to reestablish this connection, revive intimacy, and strengthen the bond that makes your relationship special.

Activities / Duration:

1. **Conversation about Dreams and Aspirations (45 minutes):**
   - Take uninterrupted time for sharing your deepest dreams, aspirations, and goals with each other. This isn't about finding solutions or making plans; rather, it's about truly comprehending each other's innermost desires and building a stronger connection.

2. **Breaking Down Barriers Session (50 minutes):**
   - Reflect on anything that might be hindering intimacy between you both. Is it work-related stress? Past traumas? Health issues? Discuss these barriers openly and brainstorm ways to navigate through them or lessen their impact.

3. **Date Night – A Walk Down Memory Lane (Takes about 2-3 hours):**
   - Plan an evening together. You could revisit the spot where you had your first date, watch the movie that started it all, or recreate a cherished memory. The idea is to relive those moments of connection.

4. **Activities for Physical Closeness (Takes about 1 hour):**
   - Engage in activities that bring you closer. It can be as simple as sharing a hug, dancing in your living room, or exchanging massages. Physical touch can be a way to reignite intimacy.

5. **Deep Emotional Sharing Session (Lasts around 40 minutes):**
   - Share something with each other that you've never revealed before. It could be a childhood memory, a fear, or a hidden talent. The goal is to encourage vulnerability and deepen your bond.

Tips for Engaging with Your Partner:

- **Prioritize Quality Time:** Ensure the time you allocate for these activities is free from distractions. Put away your phones, resist the urge to check emails, and focus on each other.
- **Be Open and Vulnerable:** These activities require openness and vulnerability. Approach them with an open heart and a willingness to share and receive.
- **Celebrate Achievements, Big and Small:** Every step taken towards reigniting intimacy should be celebrated, regardless of how seemingly insignificant they may appear.

- **Prioritize Comfort:** While it's important to explore boundaries, it's crucial to ensure that both partners feel comfortable and at ease with the chosen activities.

Benefits:

- **Enhanced Emotional Attachment:** Sharing dreams, aspirations, and vulnerabilities can profoundly strengthen the bond between partners.
- **Revitalized Passion:** Engaging in activities that promote closeness can reignite the spark and contribute to more fulfilling physical intimacy.
- **Understanding:** Addressing obstacles to intimacy can lead to a better comprehension of each other's needs, fears, and desires.
- **Connection:** Ultimately, the purpose of this week's activities is to reinforce the bond between partners, fostering a stronger and more resilient relationship.

By the conclusion of Week 5, couples should experience a renewed sense of intimacy and connection. The activities and conversations throughout this week serve as reminders of their connection while encouraging partners to consistently nurture and cherish their relationship.

Week 6: Embracing Vulnerability

Drawing inspiration from Brené Brown's research on vulnerability, this week we'll delve into its significance within relationships. The exercises are designed to challenge both partners to open up about their fears, hopes, and dreams, fostering an emotional connection. Our goal is to embrace vulnerability as a strength rather than a weakness, creating a safe and open space for both partners to express their deepest thoughts, insecurities, hopes, and dreams. Through this process, we aim to cultivate an emotional connection between both individuals.

Activities / Duration:

1. **Vulnerability Discussion (45 minutes):**
   - Start off the week by watching a talk or reading excerpts from Brené Brown's books on vulnerability. Engage in a discussion about your

initial reactions and feelings towards vulnerability within your relationship.

2. **Fear Sharing Exercise (40 minutes):**
   - In an intimate setting, each partner will take turns sharing a fear or insecurity that they have never voiced before. The other partner is encouraged to listen without judgment and provide support.

3. **Dreams Sharing (50 minutes):**
   - Share aspirations or dreams that you have kept close to your hearts. These can range from personal goals to collective dreams for the future of your relationship.

4. **Step Outside of Comfort Zones as a Couple (Time Varies):**
   - Challenge yourselves to engage in activities together or engage in open discussions about topics you may have avoided in the past. The goal is to experience vulnerability as a team.

5. **Reflection Time (End of the Week):**
   - Set aside some time for reflection at the end of the week. Talk about how being vulnerable made you feel and discuss the impact it had on your relationship.

Tips for Engaging with Your Partner:

- **Create a Non-Judgmental Space:** Allow for genuine sharing in all discussions and activities.
- **Practice Active Listening:** Be present without rushing to provide solutions or responses when your partner opens up to you.
- **Embrace Discomfort:** Recognize discomfort as part of vulnerability, seeing it as an opportunity for personal growth.
- **Offer Words of Affirmation:** After your partner shares, reinforce trust with words of affirmation and appreciation.

Benefits of Embracing Vulnerability:
- **Emotional Connection:** Accept each other's unfettered selves with authenticity, developing a deep emotional bond.
- **Strengthened Trust:** Sharing fears and dreams showcases reliability and understanding, building a foundation of trust.
- **Personal Development:** Confronting and addressing insecurities leads to individual growth.

- **Stronger Relationships:** A relationship that encourages vulnerability is based on trust, understanding, and mutual respect.

By the end of Week 6, couples should have a renewed appreciation for the importance of vulnerability in deepening their relationship. Embracing vulnerability sets the stage for understanding, trust, and an unbreakable bond. It serves as a reminder that by showing our true selves, we allow our relationships to flourish.

Week 7: Building Trust through Activities

This week is dedicated to rebuilding or strengthening trust in your relationship. The activities are designed to encourage partners to rely on each other and to engage in conversations about past betrayals and the journey towards healing.

Focus and Objective of the Week: The focus of this week is on the critical aspect of any relationship: trust. After exploring the dynamics of vulnerability, effective communication, and emotional connection, it's time to concentrate on activities that can mend broken trust or reinforce existing trust. The aim is to establish a foundation where both partners feel secure, valued, and confident in each other's commitment.

Activities / Duration:

1. **Trust Fall Exercise (20 minutes):**
   - A classic activity that fosters trust. One partner falls backward while relying on the other to catch them, symbolizing the reliance you have on one another.
2. **Open Conversations about Past Betrayals (1 hour):**
   - Engage in non-confrontational conversations about past actions that may have caused hurt or harm, focusing on understanding the emotions involved and seeking a path towards healing.
3. **Blindfolded Partner Activity (45 minutes):**
   - One person wears a blindfold while the other guides them through a path or obstacle course, highlighting the significance of guidance, active listening, and reliance on each other.
4. **Writing Letters of Commitment (1 hour):**

- Individually compose letters expressing your commitment, understanding of past mistakes, and envisioning rebuilding trust in the future. Discuss these letters together.
5. **Reflection and Future Planning Session (40 minutes):**
   - Reflect on the trust-building activities throughout the week, discuss your emotions, any realizations, and formulate plans to ensure that trust remains a focus in your relationship.

Tips for Engaging as Partners:

- **Patience is Key:** Building trust takes time. Be patient with each other, especially when discussing betrayals.
- **Active Participation:** Engage fully in all activities. The true value lies in the emotions and intentions behind them.
- **Honesty:** Share your feelings and concerns openly. This week is dedicated to establishing a foundation of trust, relying heavily on honesty.
- **Reassurance:** Show your partner that you're committed to them, especially after deep conversations about past issues.

Benefits:

- **Strengthened Relationship Foundation:** Trust solidifies the foundation of any relationship.
- **Enhanced Emotional Security:** As trust grows, both partners feel emotionally secure and know they can rely on each other.
- **Conflict Reduction:** A relationship built on trust tends to have fewer conflicts due to less room for doubt and misunderstandings.
- **Deeper Intimacy:** Trust enhances intimacy as partners feel safe enough to share their feelings, desires, and fears.

By the end of Week 7, couples should experience a renewed sense of trust in each other. This week serves as a reminder that broken trust can be rebuilt with care and become the driving force behind a strong, intimate relationship.

Week 8: Fun and Playfulness

Bring back fun and playfulness into the relationship by introducing light-hearted activities. Whether it's exploring a hobby together, playing board games, or simply reminiscing about enjoyable memories, make sure this week is filled with laughter and joy. The main focus this week is to bring back the joy and fun that often gets overshadowed by our daily routines and responsibilities. The primary goal is to remind couples of the playful side of their relationship, share laughter, and create new happy memories together.

Here are some activities you can try:

1. **Taking a Trip Down Memory Lane (1 hour):**
   - Sit down together and revisit photos, videos, or keepsakes. Reminisce about past times, vacations, funny moments, and spontaneous adventures you've had.

2. **Having a Board Game Night (2 hours):**
   - Dust off those board games and challenge each other! Whether it's a strategy game, a game of chance, or a simple card game, the aim is to have fun and be playful.

3. **Exploring a Hobby (3 hours):**
   - Always been curious about pottery? Perhaps dancing or trying out a new cuisine? Choose a hobby that interests both of you and give it a shot. It's not about being perfect at it, but rather enjoying the experience together.

4. **Enjoying a Comedy Movie Marathon (3 hours):**
   - Pick a couple of your favorite comedy movies or discover new ones that tickle your funny bone. These activities are designed to reignite joy in your relationship by embracing playfulness and creating shared moments. Let's gather some snacks, get comfy, and enjoy some laughter.

5. **Outdoor Fun Activity (2 hours):**
   - Depending on what you enjoy, we can have a picnic in the park, fly kites, or even have a water balloon fight. The goal is to be outside and have a great time.

Dedicated Tips for Engaging as Partners:
- **Stay Open-Minded:** Some activities may seem silly or unfamiliar to you. Embrace them with an open heart and mind.

- **No Heavy Discussions:** Let's avoid heavy conversations during these activities this week. The focus is on having fun.
- **Be Fully Present:** Engage wholeheartedly in the activity, leaving distractions like phones or work concerns behind.
- **Celebrate Victories:** If we try a new hobby or game, let's celebrate even the smallest achievements, like successfully trying out a new recipe without burning down the kitchen.

Benefits:
- **Stress Reduction:** Laughter and play naturally help reduce stress. This week will be an opportunity for both of us to relax and unwind.
- **Reconnection:** Engaging in fun activities together can reignite our connection and remind us why we fell in love.
- **Creating Memories:** Every activity presents an opportunity to make memories that we hold dear.
- **Strengthened Connection:** Sharing experiences, especially enjoyable ones, strengthens the bond between partners.

By the conclusion of Week 8, couples should feel a renewed connection, having shared moments filled with pure happiness and laughter. This week reminds us of the importance of making space for fun and cherishing the moments in our relationship amidst the challenges, responsibilities, and routines.

Week 9: Managing Finances and Building Trust
Money often becomes a topic in relationships that leads to conflicts. This week, let's dedicate our time to having honest discussions about our financial goals, responsibilities, and any existing conflicts. To help us collaborate effectively, we can seek guidance from counselors or use budgeting apps to create a joint financial plan.

Focus and Objectives for the Week:
This week, we will address one of the key areas of tension in relationships: finances. Our goal is to encourage communication about our individual financial aspirations, responsibilities, and any disagreements related to money matters. By the end of this week, we aim to gain an understanding of our joint financial situation and develop a roadmap for future planning.

Suggested Activities Description and Duration:

1. **Creating a Financial Vision Board (2 hours):**
   - Let's start by creating a vision board that represents both of our goals. We can include dreams like buying a home, traveling together, or saving for retirement. This activity will help us visualize our shared future.

2. **Having an Open Financial Discussion (1.5 hours):**
   - It's important for us to take some time to openly discuss any concerns, debts, or goals we may have individually or as a couple. During this conversation, let's focus on understanding each other's perspectives without judgment or criticism.

3. **Budgeting Workshop (2-hour session):**
   - Collaborate using budgeting apps or traditional methods to create an annual budget. Be sure to cover savings, expenses, and any plans for debt repayment.

4. **Financial Counseling Session (1-hour consultation):**
   - Consider scheduling a session with a counselor or advisor who can offer valuable insights into your financial planning and address any specific concerns you may have.

5. **Allocation of Responsibilities (1-hour discussion):**
   - Engage in a conversation to determine who will take charge of financial tasks, such as bill payments, investment management, or tracking savings. This promotes clarity and shared responsibility.

Valuable Tips for Increasing Partner Involvement:

- **Stay Calm and Open:** Money-related discussions can sometimes be sensitive. Approach conversations with an open-minded attitude and maintain composure.
- **Learn Together:** If one partner has more financial knowledge, view it as an opportunity for both of you to expand your understanding as a team. Share resources, like books or articles, that can educate both individuals.

- **Celebrate Milestones, Big or Small:** Take the time to acknowledge and celebrate achievements, whether it's successfully sticking to the budget for a month or saving money.
- **Seek External Support When Needed:** If financial discussions become intense or difficult to navigate, don't hesitate to seek mediation or counseling services.

Benefits:
- **Having a Vision for Your Financial Future:** By visualizing and discussing goals together, couples can align their aspirations and ensure they're on the same financial page.
- **Reduction in Financial Stress:** Open communication and careful planning can significantly decrease anxieties and uncertainties surrounding finances when couples work together to manage their money.
- **Strengthening the Partnership:** Managing finances jointly fosters teamwork and shared responsibility, creating a bond within the relationship.

By the end of Week 9, couples should have developed a shared vision for their goals. This week focuses on emphasizing the importance of teamwork in managing finances and highlights how open communication and planning can bring a sense of security. Another empowering aspect is having a defined plan, allowing couples to feel more empowered and in control of their financial journey.

Week 10: Planning for the Future

This week is about engaging in conversations regarding long-term objectives, including family planning and career aspirations. It's a time to understand each other's dreams and explore ways to support one another in achieving them. The focus is on aligning your visions for the future.

Focus and Objective of the Week: This week is dedicated to envisioning a future together. From aspirations to shared goals, the aim is to comprehend, appreciate, and provide backing for each other's long-term ambitions. By the end of the week, couples should have a roadmap for their future endeavors, ensuring that both partners feel valued and understood in their pursuits.

Description and Duration of Activities:

- **Mapping Dreams (2 hours):**
  - Record personal and shared dreams for the next 5, 10, and 20 years. These may encompass career advancements, travel aspirations, family planning, or personal growth objectives. Then, share these dreams with each other and engage in discussions.
- **Workshop on Support System (1.5 hours):**
  - Explore how each partner can provide support to help accomplish dreams. Here are some suggestions for improving your relationship and planning for the future.
- **Communication and Compromise (2 hours):**
  - Discuss the importance of compromise, encouragement, and being open to tangible steps like relocating for a partner's job opportunity.
- **Family Planning Session (2 hours):**
  - Have an open conversation about expanding your family. Consider topics such as the number of children you both desire, parenting philosophies, and timelines.
- **Career Aspirations Discussion (1.5 hours):**
  - Share your individual career goals, potential challenges ahead, and explore ways to support each other in your professional journeys.
- **Creating a Joint Vision Board (2 hours):**
  - Based on the dreams and goals you've discussed, create a visual representation of your shared future using a joint vision board. This will serve as a reminder of the steps needed to achieve those dreams together.

Tips for Engaging with Your Partner:

- **Practice Listening:** When your partner shares their dreams or concerns.
- **Be Open to Compromises:** As you align your visions for the future.
- **Celebrate Each Other's Achievements:** And milestones.

- **Understand That Dreams and Plans Can Evolve:** Be willing to revisit them periodically and make adjustments accordingly.

Overall, it's important to maintain communication, flexibility, and mutual support as you navigate through life together. Make it a habit to regularly revisit these discussions.

Advantages:

- **Unified Vision:** By discussing and aligning on goals, couples can move forward with a shared vision.
- **Deepened Connection:** Understanding and supporting each other's dreams fosters a stronger emotional bond.
- **Clarity and Purpose:** Having a clear roadmap for the future provides direction and purpose in the relationship.
- **Mutual Support:** This week emphasizes the importance of being each other's supporter, reinforcing the strength of the partnership.

By the end of Week 10, couples should feel more in sync with their aspirations, understanding how they can support each other in achieving their dreams. This week showcases the power of support and shared visions in strengthening the bond between partners.

Week 11: Looking Back and Sharing Feedback

This week is an opportunity to reflect on the progress made over the past ten weeks. Share what worked, what didn't, and identify areas that still need attention. Let's celebrate our achievements and set goals for the coming weeks.

Focus and Goal for This Week: The main objective this week is reflection and evaluation. Our goal is to assess the journey thus far, recognizing the milestones we've achieved, acknowledging the challenges we've faced, and setting a positive direction for our future. By the end of this week, we should understand our growth areas and have a renewed commitment to our relationship journey.

Description of Activities and Duration:
1. **Reviewing Our Journey (2 hours):**

- Spend time together discussing both the highlights and low points of the past ten weeks. Reflect on activities that brought joy, ones that were challenging, and moments of valuable insight.

2. **Sharing Feedback (1.5 hours):**
   - Share feedback with each other in a hearted manner. Discuss your partner's strengths and what they did well, as well as areas where they could provide more support or understanding.

3. **Celebrating Achievements (1 hour):**
   - Celebrate all our milestones, no matter how small. It can be as simple as having dinner at home or exchanging small tokens of appreciation with each other.

4. **Setting Goals Session (2 hours):**
   - After reflecting and receiving feedback, take some time to set goals for the coming weeks. These goals can include continuing activities, taking on new challenges, or focusing on areas that need improvement.

5. **Renewing Commitment (1 hour):**
   - Take a moment to reaffirm your commitment to each other and your relationship. This can be done through affirmations, writing letters to one another, or any other symbolic gesture that holds meaning for both of you.

Helpful Tips for Engaging with Your Partner:

- **Maintain a Positive Approach:** Emphasize positive aspects when providing feedback, viewing challenges as opportunities for growth rather than criticism.
- **Be Open and Receptive:** Listen without becoming defensive when receiving feedback. Remember, it's intended to enhance your relationship.
- **Celebrate Small Achievements:** Every accomplishment, no matter how small, is a step forward. Take the time to celebrate them.
- **Stay Committed:** Recall the reasons why you embarked on this journey together and renew your dedication to one another.

Benefits Couples Can Expect from Engaging in This Program:

- **Gain Understanding:** Reflecting on the past weeks allows couples to gain insights into the dynamics of their relationship, leading to a better understanding of each other.
- **Find a Path Forward:** By identifying what has worked and what hasn't, couples can make informed decisions about their future together.
- **Strengthen the Bond:** Celebrating achievements and reaffirming commitments helps strengthen the connection between partners.
- **Boost Motivation:** Setting goals for the weeks ahead provides motivation and a sense of purpose in the relationship.

As we conclude Week 11, couples should feel revitalized and focused on their journey. The process of reflection, feedback, and goal setting ensures that their relationship continues to grow, evolve, and become stronger as they pave the way for an enriching partnership.

Week 12: Commitment and Renewal

Wrap up the therapy plan by recommitting yourselves to each other. Consider renewing your vows, writing love letters, or simply having open conversations about your shared future. Embrace this opportunity to celebrate your strengthened bond and embrace a future together.

Focus and Goal of the Week: This final week marks the culmination of our 12-week journey. It's about celebrating your deepened connection while looking ahead with hope and dedication for what lies ahead. The main goal is to reinforce love, trust, and commitment to one another, ensuring that the relationship continues to thrive.

Activities/Duration:

1. **Sharing Heartfelt Letters (2 hours):**
   - Set aside a peaceful time to write sincere letters to each other. Reflect on the past, express gratitude for the present, and share hopes for the future. Exchange these letters and read them aloud together.
2. **Renewing Vows Ceremony (3 hours):**
   - Consider renewing your vows in a simple ceremony at home or a more elaborate event with close friends and family. It's an

opportunity to reaffirm your promises and celebrate your journey so far.

3. **Strolling Down Memory Lane (2 hours):**
   - Take a leisurely walk down memory lane together. Visit places that hold significance, such as where you first met or had your first date. Reminisce about the moments that have brought you closer.

4. **Mapping Out the Future (2 hours):**
   - Engage in meaningful discussions about future plans, setting relationship goals, and envisioning adventures you would like to experience together. This could involve discussing travel plans, establishing family objectives, or sharing aspirations.

5. **Ritual of Commitment (1 hour):**
   - Come up with a ritual that symbolizes your renewed commitment. It could be something like planting a tree, attaching a love padlock to a bridge, or any other meaningful gesture.

Valuable Tips for Partners:
- **Be Authentic:** When writing letters or renewing vows, speak from the heart and let your genuine emotions shine through.
- **Treasure the Moments:** As you reminisce about the past, cherish the memories and acknowledge how far you've come.
- **Dream Together:** When envisioning the future, dare to dream and ensure that both partners' dreams and aspirations are taken into account.
- **Stay Present:** During the commitment ritual, fully immerse yourself in the moment, understanding its significance.

Benefits:
- **Connection:** The activities during this week aim to deepen the bond between partners even further.
- **Clear Path for the Future:** By planning together, you gain clarity and establish a shared vision for your journey ahead.
- **Revitalized Romance:** Exchanging love letters and renewing vows reignite passion and romance within the relationship.
- **Sense of Accomplishment:** Reflecting on your 12-week journey brings a sense of achievement as you acknowledge all the effort put in and celebrate progress made.

As we wrap up Week 12, it's important for couples to feel a sense of connection, commitment, and optimism. The activities and reflections from this week lay the groundwork for growth, understanding, and love, ensuring that the relationship flourishes in the days ahead.

Discovering the Magic of Your Weekly Therapy Plan

Embarking on this therapy plan is akin to setting sail on a vast ocean alongside your partner. The waves, tides, sunsets, and storms all symbolize the array of emotions and experiences that lie ahead. Here's how you can make this journey truly transformative:

1. **Plan Your Path Together:** Prior to delving into each week's activities, take a moment with your partner. Create an atmosphere with some candlelight and soft music while discussing your aspirations and dreams for the upcoming week. Remember, this is an adventure you embark on together; synchronize your compasses.

2. **Cherish Your Time:** Amidst the busyness of life, it can be easy to let precious moments slip away unnoticed. However, envision each therapy activity as a treasure waiting to be discovered on a map. Dedicate time to unearth these gems. You'll be rewarded with deeper emotional connections.

3. **Embrace the Unknown:** Some weeks may feel like sailing through waters where topics arise that evoke strong emotions. Hold each other's hands, take a breath, and venture into these depths together. The treasures of knowledge and understanding that await you are truly invaluable.

4. **Speak from the Heart:** Let your emotions guide your communication. When an experience stirs feelings within you, express them openly. Allow your partner to witness your vulnerabilities, fears, and dreams. It is in these moments that genuine bonds are formed.

5. **Embrace Life's Challenges:** Not every day will be smooth sailing. Instead of waiting for difficult times to pass, learn to embrace them as opportunities for growth together. Celebrate the moments of joy, share laughter, and exchange meaningful glances even amidst life's storms.

6. **Seek Support from Your Circle:** If the journey becomes overwhelming, remember that you are not alone in this voyage. Seek guidance from trusted therapists and wise friends. Rely on a supportive community who can lend a helping hand.

7. **Stay Rooted in Commitment:** Despite the challenges that may arise along the way, always remember the promises you made to one another. The anchor of commitment will keep you grounded when turbulent waves attempt to steer you off course.

8. **Cherish Moments of Serenity:** At the end of each week, find a tranquil spot where you can marvel at a sunset and reflect upon your shared experiences. Let's talk about the experiences you've had, the challenges you've overcome, and the exciting new horizons you're eager to explore.

With these strategies, your weekly therapy plan goes beyond just a list of activities. It becomes a journey for both hearts involved—a dance of emotions and a promise of love that deepens with each passing moment.

Dear Reader

I genuinely hope that this book has offered you insights and advice on how to cultivate a relationship.

As an independent author your input is incredibly valuable to me.

Your opinion holds importance so I kindly request you to consider writing an honest review. By following this link, it will directly take you to the Amazon reviewing page:

https://www.amazon.com/review/create-review/?asin=**B0CJSYZW57**

Will only take around 30 seconds of your time.

Thank you sincerely for your support.

Warmest regards,

Esther Collins

Part III: Strategies for Building Strong Relationships

Delving into the Depths of Intimacy; Emotional versus Physical Bond

Intimacy, a concept often whispered among couples, forms the foundation of a profound and fulfilling relationship. But what does it truly entail? Is it the warmth that radiates from a touch, the profound connection forged through heartfelt conversations, or the vulnerability shared in revealing secrets? Intimacy encompasses both physical and emotional dimensions, but how do these aspects intertwine, and how can couples navigate this intricate dance?

Emotional Intimacy: The Subtle Language of the Heart

Intimacy speaks volumes without uttering a word. It is the solace of knowing someone will catch you when you stumble, the delight of sharing laughter through jokes, and finding comfort in leaning on someone's shoulder during challenging times. This level of closeness is built upon trust, understanding, and mutual respect. How does one nurture such a deep bond?

The key to fostering intimacy lies in open communication. Sharing dreams, fears, and aspirations paves the way for comprehension between partners. However, have you ever wondered why sharing brings about immense satisfaction? What causes us to feel connected when we reveal ourselves to another person? Because in those moments, it's not about exchanging words; it's about sharing a piece of your innermost self. When two souls connect, their bond becomes unbreakable.

Physical Intimacy: More Than Skin Deep

Speaking of intimacy, it is the tangible manifestation of love and affection. It goes beyond mere instances and encompasses gentle caresses, spontaneous hugs, and comforting cuddles. Is physical intimacy merely superficial? Think back to the last time you held your partner's hand. What did it convey? Security? Love? Reassurance? Physical gestures, no matter how small, carry a multitude of emotions. They are the language that fills the gaps between conversations. How can couples ensure that their physical connection remains strong and meaningful?

It is crucial to remember that physical intimacy is an extension of the bond. When emotional closeness flourishes, every touch and every glance becomes infused with significance. So how can you ensure that your physical connection remains as deep as your emotional one?

Bridging Emotional and Physical Intimacy

Building a bridge between emotional and physical intimacy relies on mutual respect, understanding, and continuous effort. It's important to recognize the needs of your partner and make them feel valued, both emotionally and physically. How often do you truly take a moment to understand your partner's desires, fears, and dreams? When was the last time you showed your love through actions rather than just words?

Relationships are like gardens that require nurturing. Both emotional and physical intimacy act as the water that nourishes them. By understanding the intricacies of both forms of intimacy, couples can ensure their relationship remains vibrant and fulfilling.

As you navigate through stages of your relationship, ask yourself; Are you tending to both the heart and senses? How can you deepen your bond to ensure that emotional and physical intimacy flourish harmoniously? Remember, in the dance of love, both forms of intimacy play a role. When they are in sync, it creates nothing short of magic.

Exploring Intimacy: Activities to Overcome Barriers

Intimacy is the foundation of a thriving relationship, balancing emotional and physical connections. Yet, sometimes obstacles arise that can shadow this bond. The true beauty lies in overcoming these obstacles, rediscovering the closeness that was once present, or even finding a deeper connection than ever before.

1. **The Vision Board for Intimacy**
   - **How to do it:**
     - Gather magazines, photographs, or printouts that resonate with your emotions regarding intimacy.
     - Collaboratively create a vision board while discussing the significance of each chosen image or word.

2. The Power of Silent Connection
- **How to do it:**
  - Sit facing each other, maintaining eye contact while holding hands.
  - Without speaking, express your emotions through your eyes and touch. This method connects without the barrier of language.

3. The Playlist for Intimacy
- **How to do it:**
  - Each partner curates a playlist consisting of songs that remind them of stages in their relationship or songs that express their sentiments about intimacy.
  - Spend an evening together listening to these playlists, engaging in discussions about the memories or emotions each song evokes.

4. The Gratitude Jar
- **How to do it:**
  - Keep a jar and some pieces of paper handy. Every day, write down something you appreciate about your partner and put it in the jar.
  - At the end of each month, take time to read those notes together. It's a way to cherish the small things that often go unnoticed.

5. The Touch Map
- **How to do it:**
  - Use a body outline or simply have a conversation about which areas of your body you enjoy being touched and which areas are more sensitive or ticklish.
  - This is an insightful way to learn about each other's physical desires.

6. The Future Projection Exercise
- **How to do it:**
  - Sit down together and talk about where you envision yourselves in 5, 10, or 20 years from now.
  - Visualize aspects like your future home, travel plans, or even family dynamics. This exercise helps align your dreams and aspirations.

Remember, intimacy is a journey that evolves and grows over time. These activities are suggestions to help deepen your understanding and connection with your partner. As you engage in these activities, remember that intimacy is about the moments you share, the unspoken understanding, and the respect you have for each other. What layers will you uncover in your relationship today?

Understanding Significant Life Transitions
Significant life transitions can occur in various forms, whether planned or unexpected. These transitions encompass a range of experiences, from new beginnings to unforeseen obstacles. Regardless of the nature of these changes, approaching them as a team can strengthen your resilience and unity.

Step 1: Open and Transparent Communication When faced with times of change, prioritizing honest communication becomes crucial. It's important to express your thoughts, concerns, and aspirations with one another. Actively listen to each other and create a safe space where your partner feels comfortable sharing their emotions.

Step 2: Acknowledge Emotions Change often stirs up a mixture of emotions, ranging from excitement to anxiety. Recognize that both you and your partner may experience these emotions differently. Show patience and empathy towards each other's feelings.

Step 3: Embrace Adaptability Being flexible is essential when confronted with the unknown. Be willing to adjust your plans and expectations as circumstances evolve. Approaching change with an open mind helps alleviate stress and fosters unity.

Step 4: Cultivate a Supportive Atmosphere Offer support to one another during times of transition. Be each other's cheerleader by providing encouragement and reassurance. Knowing that you have a partner who believes in you can make challenges feel more manageable.

Step 5: Seek Opportunities for Personal Growth Every challenge presents an opportunity for growth, both on an individual level and within your relationship. Use life changes as an opportunity to discover more about yourselves and one another. Engage in conversations about the lessons you're learning and the strengths you're uncovering.

Embracing Parenthood and Adjusting to Family Changes

The arrival of a new family member, whether through childbirth or adoption, brings both joy and the need for adaptation. It's a period for growth as you embrace parenthood together while navigating changes in your family dynamics.

Discussing Parenting Values and Expectations

- Before your child arrives, discuss your parenting values, expectations, and roles with your partner. Understanding each other's approach to parenting is crucial for teamwork.
- Create a partnership by sharing parenting responsibilities. Support each other through the ups and downs of raising a child.

Maintaining Connection as a Couple

- Even as you transition into parenthood, it's important to maintain your connection as a couple.
- Set aside time for date nights and meaningful conversations to nurture your relationship.

Facing Life's Challenges Together

- Life can present challenges that test the strength of your relationship, such as health issues, financial setbacks, or unforeseen circumstances.
- During these times, rely on each other for emotional support. Listen, provide comfort, and remind each other that you're in this journey together.
- Approach challenges as a team by collaborating on solutions. Teamwork can help you overcome any obstacle.

Seeking Help When Overwhelmed

- If challenges become overwhelming, don't hesitate to seek help.
- Couples counseling or therapy can provide tools for navigating adversity effectively.

Establishing a Strong Base for Endurance

- Life alterations are crucial turning points, and how you handle them greatly influences the course of your relationship.
- By embracing challenges through dialogue, adaptability, and shared encouragement, you're not just enduring difficult times but also

constructing a solid groundwork of resilience that will support you in forthcoming changes.

- Remember, change is inevitable, but the bond between you and your partner can remain unwavering throughout it all.

In summary, navigating the transition to parenthood and adjusting to family changes requires open communication, shared responsibility, maintaining your connection as a couple, facing challenges together, and seeking external support when needed. By doing so, you're laying a strong foundation for a resilient and enduring relationship.

Dealing with Conflict #1; Handling Financial Stress

Financial stress can often sneak into relationships uninvited, causing tension and exposing vulnerabilities. Whether you're facing a setback, managing different spending habits, or making significant monetary decisions, money matters can be a source of conflict. However, approaching this stress as a team can transform it into an opportunity for growth.

Understanding the Impact of Financial Stress

- Financial stress can strain even the most robust relationships. Recognizing its impact on both partners and addressing it proactively is crucial.

Open Communication

- Initiate honest conversations about your financial situation. Create a space where both partners can openly express their concerns, fears, and aspirations regarding money.

Establish Common Goals

- Set shared goals that align with both of your individual aspirations and the vision you have for your partnership. Collaboratively establishing these goals fosters a sense of unity and purpose.

Develop a Realistic Budget

- Work together to create a practical budget that ensures your financial decisions align with your goals. A budget serves as a roadmap, enabling you to make informed choices.

Clearly Define Roles and Responsibilities

- Clearly define each partner's roles and responsibilities in managing finances. Assign tasks based on each person's strengths and interests.

- Maintain transparency in financial matters. Regularly share updates about income, expenses, and any changes in the financial situation.

Dealing with Differing Spending Habits

- Embrace differences in spending habits and find a way to manage money together.
- Understanding each other's perspective plays a role. Acknowledge that each partner has their own financial mindset shaped by upbringing and experiences. By recognizing these differences, empathy can be fostered.

Finding Common Ground Through Compromise

- When making financial decisions as a couple, find common ground through compromise. Seek solutions that honor both partners' preferences while achieving shared goals.
- Agreeing on spending limits for expenses can be beneficial. Setting predefined limits helps prevent overspending and reduces potential conflicts.

Long-term Impact of Decisions

- Consider the long-term impact of financial decisions on your goals and aspirations.
- Evaluate how each decision aligns with your long-term vision.

Seeking Professional Advice

- In dealing with financial matters, it may be beneficial to seek advice from financial advisors or professionals who can offer expertise and guidance.

Active Participation and Open Communication

- It's important for both partners to actively participate and communicate openly in order to manage stress effectively. By acknowledging challenges and working together to develop strategies for handling them, you are not only managing financial stress but also building a solid foundation for your financial partnership.

Remember, the strength of your journey together is not solely determined by figures but by the trust, respect, and unity you foster in the face of financial challenges.

Handling Conflict #2: Healing from Infidelity

One particular aspect of conflict resolution involves healing from infidelity. Infidelity is a breach of trust that has the potential to deeply impact a relationship's foundation. The process of healing from infidelity is one that requires both partners to navigate through a complex range of emotions and confront painful truths. Ultimately, it necessitates making decisions about whether to rebuild or part ways. Although healing may appear daunting at first glance, it's crucial to keep in mind that couples equipped with appropriate tools and genuinely committed to change can emerge stronger and more resilient from this painful experience.

However, in the midst of this situation, there is an opportunity for healing, personal growth, and a deeper level of understanding. This can only happen if we approach it with genuine empathy.

Empathy in this context goes beyond justifying or ignoring the act. It involves comprehending the underlying emotions, motivations, and vulnerabilities that contributed to it. It's about listening without judgment, empathizing with the pain experienced by all parties involved, and working together towards the path of healing.

Before embarking on the journey of healing, it's crucial to understand why infidelity occurred in the first place. Was it a lapse in judgment? A search for connection? Perhaps an attempt to escape from relationship monotony? While we cannot change what happened, understanding its causes can lay the foundation for genuine comprehension.

To illustrate this point further, let's consider the story of Elena and Mark. Feeling neglected and emotionally distant from Mark, Elena sought solace in the attention she received from a coworker. It wasn't about seeking excitement or novelty; rather, it was driven by a void within her marriage. When Mark discovered the affair, his initial reaction was one of anger and betrayal. As they went deeper into their journey, aided by therapy, they came to realize the underlying problems in their relationship that had been neglected for far too long.

Recognizing and Preventing Infidelity; A Comprehensive Insight

While infidelity can stem from complex reasons, understanding its early signs and taking proactive measures can help couples protect their relationship. Here is a detailed analysis of identifying the indicators and preventing infidelity.

1. Emotional Disconnect: One of the precursors to infidelity is feeling emotionally disconnected. When partners sense a lack of intimacy, they may seek it elsewhere. This doesn't always result in physical betrayal but can manifest as an emotional affair.

Prevention Tip: Regularly check in with one another. Engage in communication about emotions, concerns, and needs to bridge any emotional gaps. Prioritize quality time together amidst busy schedules.

2. Decreased Physical Intimacy: While it's natural for the frequency of intimacy to fluctuate in a relationship, an extended decline could be a red flag. It might indicate underlying issues or emotional disconnection.

Prevention Tip: To address the causes of decreased intimacy, it's important to have open discussions about therapy options or make efforts to reignite the spark in your relationship.

Heightened Secrecy: If your partner starts becoming more secretive about their actions, phone usage, or social media behavior, it might be a cause for concern. While everyone deserves privacy, a significant change in behavior should catch your attention.

Prevention Tip: Foster an environment of trust and openness. Instead of resorting to snooping or prying, try initiating a conversation where you can discuss the observed changes.

Changes in Routine: Unexpected alterations in patterns, such as late nights at work or unexplained absences, could potentially suggest infidelity. However, it's essential to approach this situation with an open mind as there could be other reasons for these changes.

Prevention Tip: Maintain lines of communication with your partner. By discussing any reasons behind the changes in routine, you can prevent misunderstandings from arising.

Emotional Distance: When a partner becomes emotionally distant or indifferent, it may indicate that they are channeling their emotions elsewhere.

Prevention Tip: Engage in activities that nurture the connection between you and your partner. This can be as simple as planning date nights or even considering couples therapy.

Signs of Defensive Behavior: If your partner consistently reacts defensively during discussions about friends or activities, it may indicate that something is wrong.

Prevention Tip: Approach these topics with empathy. Avoid making accusations. Creating an environment for honest conversations can help prevent defensiveness from arising.

Reduced Commitment to the Relationship: If one partner seems less invested in the future of the relationship or avoids discussing long-term plans, it could suggest a wavering level of dedication.

Prevention Tip: Regularly engage in conversations and reassess relationship goals. Ensure that both partners are on the same page regarding their future together.

It's important to note that these signs do not serve as proof of infidelity. Jumping to conclusions without evidence can further strain the relationship. Instead, focus on building trust, fostering communication, and mutual respect. Additionally, it's crucial to recognize that infidelity often stems from issues within the relationship itself. Addressing these root causes can be more effective than looking out for signs of betrayal. Engaging in couples therapy, having conversations, and making mutual efforts to strengthen your bond can significantly contribute to preventing infidelity and nurturing a healthy and fulfilling relationship.

Understanding the Impact of Cheating

Cheating can have an emotional impact on both partners involved. The feelings of pain, anger, betrayal, and confusion that come with such a situation often make couples question if it's even possible to rebuild their relationship.

Rebuilding trust begins with communication. Both partners need to be open to having conversations about the affair, including the emotions that arose from it.

1. Taking Responsibility The partner who engaged in cheating must fully acknowledge their actions and accept responsibility for them. It's crucial for them to understand the pain they caused and genuinely express remorse as a step towards healing.

2. Seeking Professional Support Recovering from infidelity often requires guidance from a therapist or counselor. These trained professionals can create a space for open dialogue and offer valuable tools to navigate the complex emotions involved.

3. Rebuilding Trust Rebuilding trust is a process that cannot be rushed. The partner who committed infidelity must consistently demonstrate efforts

through their actions, proving that they are worthy of trust again, rather than just relying on words alone.

4. Self-Reflection Both partners should engage in self-reflection to understand the factors that contributed to the infidelity. By exploring these issues, they can work together to prevent such situations from arising in the future.

The Path Towards Forgiveness

Forgiveness is a personal decision and an integral part of recovering from infidelity. It is crucial to differentiate between forgiving and accepting or condoning the behavior itself.

Reestablishing Trust: A Journey, Not an Endpoint

Trust forms the foundation of any relationship. However, when it is shattered, it often leaves behind doubt, pain, and uncertainty. Rebuilding the bond between partners requires more than just quick fixes; it is a continuous journey of understanding, patience, and commitment. It involves reshaping the dynamics of the relationship and finding a balance.

Expressing Emotions

After experiencing betrayal, both partners may be overwhelmed by a whirlwind of emotions. It is crucial to create an environment where these feelings can be openly expressed without fear of judgment. Whether it's the pain caused by betrayal, the guilt of wrongdoing, or the apprehension about what lies ahead, every emotion is valid. By acknowledging and comprehending these emotions, couples lay the groundwork for healing.

Choosing Forgiveness

Forgiveness should not be seen as a sign of weakness, nor as an act of forgetting. Instead, it is a decision to let go of resentment and move forward. However, it's important to recognize that forgiveness is deeply personal. The partner who has been hurt embarks on this journey willingly when they feel ready to release their pain. Ultimately, forgiveness becomes a gift they give themselves rather than solely for their partner.

Time

The scars left by betrayal cannot be healed overnight; they gradually fade away with time, patience, and consistent effort. It's crucial for both partners to understand this reality. When someone breaks trust in a relationship, it's important for them to genuinely show remorse and a commitment to change. At the same time, the betrayed partner should allow themselves the space and time to heal without feeling pressured by external factors.

Reestablishing Intimacy

Betrayal often creates a gap in a relationship, making intimacy difficult. However, intimacy, both emotional and physical, can serve as a bridge that brings couples together again. It involves rediscovering each other, understanding vulnerabilities, and creating moments of connection. This renewed intimacy may be different from what it was but has the potential to be deeper and more meaningful.

Finding the Positive

While betrayal causes pain, it also presents an opportunity for couples to reassess, readjust, and rebuild their relationship. Many couples who have weathered this storm often come out stronger and more resilient. They develop an appreciation for each other as they truly understand the depths of their bond.

Esther Perel is known for her exploration of relationships and often discusses the dual nature of love and desire. She highlights that while love seeks closeness, security, and predictability; desire thrives on mystery, novelty, and uncertainty. In the process of rebuilding trust after betrayal, couples can strive to strike a balance between these two aspects. By prioritizing communication and transparency to establish security and predictability, individuals can also revive a sense of excitement and discovery by exploring previously unexplored aspects of their relationship. Essentially, when trust is broken, it may never fully return to its original state. However, this doesn't necessarily have to be viewed as a negative outcome. Similar to the art of kintsugi in Japan, where broken pottery is repaired with gold, relationships can find beauty in their imperfections. Instead of hiding the cracks, they are emphasized, representing the journey and resilience of love.

Healing After Betrayal: Accelerate Your Healing with These Effective Strategies

1. **The 60-Second Trust Reset:** In moments of doubt, take a deep breath, count to 60, and recall a time when your partner supported you. This brief exercise can help shift your focus from negative to positive thoughts.

2. **The Trust Jar Technique:** Each time you experience a moment that reinforces trust with your partner, jot it down and place it in a jar. When feeling doubtful or overwhelmed, read one of these notes to remind yourself of the positive aspects of your relationship.

3. **Mirror Talk:** Stand before a mirror, gaze into your own eyes, and affirm to yourself: "I am healing, I am worthy, and I am strong." Such affirmations can enhance your self-esteem and resilience.

4. **The Betrayal Playlist:** Compile a playlist of songs that echo your emotions. Music can be a powerful healing tool, providing solace and understanding during difficult periods.

5. **The Trust Timeline:** Construct a timeline detailing the significant moments, both good and bad, in your relationship. This helps you visualize the journey you've shared and the growth you've achieved together.

6. **Post-Betrayal Date Nights:** Set aside one night each week for reconnecting without discussing the betrayal. Focus on creating new, joyful memories together.

7. **The 'Why' Deep Dive:** Investigate the underlying reasons behind the betrayal. Was it a momentary error or a symptom of deeper issues? Understanding the root cause is crucial for healing and preventing future problems.

8. **The Gratitude Alarm:** Set a daily alarm at a random time. When it rings, pause to reflect on one aspect of your relationship for which you are thankful.

9. **The 'Rebuild Ritual':** Establish a new ritual or tradition that signifies your commitment to rebuilding trust. This could range from a regular evening walk to a special monthly outing.

10. **The Trust Mentor:** Seek advice from a couple who has successfully overcome a similar challenge. Their experience and wisdom can provide valuable perspective and hope.

Remember, healing from betrayal is a progressive journey. These tactics are intended to support and strengthen you along the way, aiding in trust restoration and fostering a resilient partnership.

Dealing with Conflict #3: Resolving Parenting Disagreements

"Conflict is inevitable in the journey of parenthood. Finding common ground is essential for your child's well-being."

Parenting is a rewarding yet challenging journey that often leads to conflicts within a relationship. The introduction of children brings responsibilities and decisions that can cause disagreements between partners. However, by approaching parenting conflicts with respect, communication, and a shared commitment to your child's well-being, you can strengthen your bond and foster a harmonious family environment.

Understanding Parenting Conflicts Parenthood involves decisions and responsibilities like sleep schedules and disciplinary approaches. It's important to recognize that different parenting styles and viewpoints stem from each partner's unique upbringing and beliefs.

1. Engage in Dialogue: The key to resolving parenting conflicts lies in having honest conversations. Create an environment where both partners can freely express their concerns, ideas, and perspectives without fear of judgment.

2. Prioritize Your Child's Well-Being: Remember that the well-being of your child should be the focal point when making decisions. When seeking solutions, it's important to prioritize what is best for your child's growth, well-being, and overall happiness.

3. Embrace the Art of Compromise: Parenting often involves finding middle ground. Be open to blending elements of both partners' parenting styles to create an approach that meets your child's needs.

4. Consider Seeking Professional Advice: If conflicts persist, seeking guidance from a parenting coach or counselor might be helpful. Consulting with a third party can provide valuable insights and strategies for effectively navigating differences.

5. Foster Understanding of Each Other's Perspectives: Each partner brings their unique experiences and beliefs into their parenting approach. Taking time to understand and empathize with each other's viewpoints can lead to more constructive discussions.

Resolving Typical Parenting Conflicts

Parenting disagreements can emerge in areas such as discipline or educational decisions. Here are strategies for resolving parenting conflicts:

1. **Addressing Discipline Differences** Disagreements regarding discipline are common. It's important to discuss and agree on consistent disciplinary approaches that consider factors like your child's age, temperament, and development stage.

2. **Managing Division of Responsibilities** Finding a balance between childcare responsibilities, household chores, and work commitments can sometimes lead to conflicts. Establishing roles and responsibilities that work for both partners and periodically reassessing them can help maintain harmony.

3. **Navigating Screen Time and Technology** Screen time and technology use have become significant topics in today's digital era. It's important to establish limits and demonstrate healthy screen habits as role models for your child.

4. **Making Educational Decisions** Making educational decisions can be challenging. Engage in research together, attend school meetings, and make choices that align with your child's learning style and individual needs.

5. **Dealing with Extended Family Involvement** Extended family involvement often brings opinions, which can sometimes lead to tensions. Setting boundaries and communicating your preferences with family members while prioritizing the needs of your immediate family is crucial.

When facing conflicts as parents, unity and collaboration are key. Presenting a united front to your child fosters a sense of security and consistency. Remember that disagreements are normal. How you resolve them teaches important lessons about communication, problem-solving, and respect to your child. By approaching parenting conflicts with empathy, open communication, and a shared commitment to your child's well-being, you can create a loving environment that benefits both your relationship as partners and the overall well-being of your family.

Dealing with Conflict #4: Overcoming Past Traumas

Addressing the shadows of the past can heal wounds and forge a future characterized by resilience and growth. Relationships can be deeply affected by the traumas that either one or both partners have experienced in their past. These traumatic experiences could be rooted in childhood, previous relationships, or challenging life events. While it can be challenging, facing these wounds together as a couple can bring about healing, personal growth, and ultimately strengthen your bond.

1. Recognizing the Impact of Past Traumas

   Past traumas can manifest in various ways within a relationship, leading to communication barriers and emotional triggers. It's crucial to acknowledge how these traumas may influence your interactions and make an effort to understand the causes of your partner's reactions and behaviors.

2. Creating a Safe Environment for Open Communication

   Establishing open communication is vital when addressing past traumas. Create a space that encourages both partners to share their experiences, emotions, and triggers without fear of judgment or dismissal.

3. Validating Each Other's Emotions

   Validation is a powerful tool for healing. Show empathy and understanding towards your partner by acknowledging their emotions and experiences. Let them know that you recognize the validity of their feelings and that you are there to support them.

4. Seeking Professional Assistance

   The process of healing from traumas often requires the guidance of a trained therapist or counselor. A professional can offer tools, techniques, and a supportive environment for both partners to navigate their individual and shared experiences.

5. Practicing Patience and Compassion

   Healing is a journey that requires patience and compassion. Understand that triggers and emotional responses might occur. Make a commitment to support each other through the highs and lows.

6. Establishing Boundaries

   In the healing process, it's important to establish boundaries that prioritize your well-being. Respect each other's limits and have open communication about what feels comfortable and safe.

Healing as a Couple

Healing from traumas as a couple involves both individual and collective efforts. Here are steps you can take together to facilitate healing and growth:

1. **Share Your Triggers:** Recognize and communicate triggers stemming from traumas. Understanding each other's triggers helps prevent emotional distress.

2. **Develop Coping Strategies:** Work together to develop strategies for managing triggers and emotional reactions. These could include breathing exercises, mindfulness practices, or seeking support from each other.

3. **Engage in Active Listening:** Practice active listening when discussing past traumas. Give your partner undivided attention, validate their feelings, and respond with empathy.

4. **Celebrate Milestones:** Rejoice in the milestones achieved during your healing journey. Acknowledge the steps you both have taken to heal, grow, and cultivate a resilient relationship.

Overcoming traumas can build resilience both individually and as a couple. The process of facing and conquering challenges strengthens your bond and creates a shared sense of accomplishment.

Healing from traumas requires courage, vulnerability, and a commitment to supporting each other. By confronting these challenges as a team, you not only strengthen your relationship but also establish a foundation of trust, understanding, and empathy. Remember, everyone's healing journey is unique; there is no one-size-fits-all approach. By fostering an environment of love, patience, and mutual support, you can build a future defined by resilience, growth, and renewed connection.

Navigating conflicts in relationships is like encountering storms on an otherwise calm sea. A significant challenge for couples is aligning different values. Values serve as our compass, guiding our beliefs and principles; they influence our decisions and actions.

When two people with different beliefs and principles come together, it's like merging streams into a flowing river—both beautiful and complex.

Relationships begin with the enchantment of shared interests, mutual attraction, and dreams of a future. However, individual values beneath the surface silently shape choices and perspectives. Divergence in values can test the strength of a relationship, and the journey to align these values often leads to transformation.

Navigating the terrain of aligning different values involves exploration, compromise, and growth. Here's how couples can navigate this journey:

1. **Embrace Diversity:** Recognize and appreciate the diversity of values within the relationship. These differences represent the uniqueness each person brings. Embrace them as opportunities for learning and growth.

2. **Maintain Open Communication:** Engage in open-minded conversations about your values without judgment. Listen attentively to each other's stories, experiences, and reasons behind your beliefs.

3. **Discover Common Ground:** Look for shared values or areas where your respective values complement each other amidst the differences. These intersections can serve as the foundation for understanding in your relationship.

4. **Prioritize Core Values:** Some values are at the core of who we are and define our identity. It's important to differentiate between these core values and those that allow for flexibility. Prioritizing core values helps resolve disagreements.

5. **Adapt and Find Common Ground:** In situations where alignment seems distant, explore ways to adapt and find common ground with your values. This doesn't mean compromising your beliefs but finding creative solutions that honor both perspectives.

6. **Cultivate Empathy:** Put yourself in each other's shoes. Understand the stories that have shaped their values. Empathy fosters a connection and respect for each other's unique journeys.

7. **Grow Together:** Relationships thrive when partners grow side by side. Use the process of aligning your values as an opportunity for individual and shared growth. Let your experiences broaden your horizons.

8. **Seek Guidance:** If conflicts persist, seeking guidance from a relationship counselor can be helpful. A skilled professional can facilitate discussions and offer strategies for navigating conflicts related to values.

Embracing the task of reconciling values is not about creating replicas but about harmonizing distinct elements into a beautiful symphony. It involves recognizing the beauty in diversity and acknowledging that shared aspirations can arise from different perspectives.

In the fabric of love, the presence of contrasting values can contribute to strength, depth, and resilience. As you embark on the path towards alignment, remember that it's not just about reaching a common destination; it's also about understanding the twists and turns that shape your partner's individual journey. The process of aligning values transforms conflicts into opportunities for intimacy and personal growth.

As you navigate through differences in values, let them guide you towards a connection. Embrace the conversations, disagreements, and growth that emerge when aligning your values. This journey may present challenges but has the potential to cultivate a relationship that is not only harmonious but uniquely magnificent—an exquisite masterpiece woven from your distinctive values, mutual understanding, and unwavering love.

Dealing with Conflict #5: Managing Challenges from Relationships

In the intricate dance of relationships, conflicts do not solely originate from within the partnership. At times, discord seeps in from the periphery, where external relationships cast their shadows over the union. Eleanor Roosevelt's insightful words, "To handle yourself, use your head; to handle others, use your heart," hold profound truth when addressing issues stemming from outside relationships. Navigating these dynamics successfully demands a delicate balance between thoughtful consideration and empathetic connection.

Our lives' tapestry is woven with threads that extend beyond our intimate connections. Friends, family members, colleagues, and acquaintances all contribute to the rich mosaic of our existence. However, the interplay between these threads and the core fabric of a romantic partnership can sometimes introduce challenges. Whether it's a friend who interferes, a family member who casts doubts, or any external influence questioning the relationship, dealing effectively with these issues requires a blend of tact and compassion.

When external relationships cast shadows upon the landscape of a couple's relationship, seeking understanding becomes paramount. Both partners must extend empathy toward each other's feelings and perspectives. The partner influenced by external sources may find themselves torn between the bond with their partner and external pressures, experiencing conflicting loyalties. On the other side, the other partner may grapple with feelings of insecurity or uncertainty, triggered by these outside intrusions. By fostering an environment for open communication, where both partners' voices are respected and attentively heard, they lay the groundwork for mutual understanding and unity.

The role of empathy in addressing issues from external relationships is paramount. When Eleanor Roosevelt advises using our hearts to handle others, she emphasizes the importance of empathy in navigating these situations. Partners must be attuned not only to their own emotions but also to the emotional landscape of their significant other. This empathy sets the stage for constructive conversations and collaborative solutions, steering clear of blame or defensiveness.

Often, external influences are rooted in a complex web of connections that have been woven over time. For instance, a friend's unsolicited opinion might be shaped by their own experiences or biases. Taking time to understand these relationships—looking beyond mere surface-level observations—can offer valuable insights into managing their impact on the romantic partnership. As Eleanor Roosevelt's wisdom suggests, employing logic and critical thinking is crucial in navigating these intricacies.

When conflicts arise from external relationships, it's critical for partners to remember they are a team facing these challenges together. Eleanor Roosevelt's words serve as a reminder that effective communication is crucial in finding resolutions. It requires partners to collaboratively develop strategies to address conflicts from external sources, all the while respecting the boundaries of their relationship and considering their broader social connections.

In facing conflicts stemming from external relationships, emotional intelligence, respect, and collaboration become indispensable. Partners need to approach these challenges with open hearts, using empathy to understand the complexities at play. Roosevelt's guidance suggests that a blend of cognitive understanding and emotional depth is necessary to navigate these dynamics. By combining these principles, partners can not only handle external conflicts but also fortify the foundation of their romantic bond. This approach helps protect the relationship from external pressures and nurtures it through understanding and connection.

Strengthening the Relationship: Commemorating Milestones and Accomplishments

In the journey of love and companionship, every progress made, regardless of its size, serves as evidence of the bond shared between partners. Recognizing and commemorating these milestones and achievements is crucial for fostering the relationship's growth and ensuring its longevity.

- **Recognizing the Significance of Celebrations:** Celebrating milestones like anniversaries, overcoming challenges together, or achieving shared goals strengthens the connection between partners. It serves as a reminder of the path taken together, the obstacles overcome, and the precious memories created. These celebrations act as moments to pause in our fast-paced lives, allowing couples to reflect on their journey together while expressing gratitude towards one another.

- **Identifying Milestones:** While anniversaries, birthdays, and holidays are commonly acknowledged milestones, it is equally important to acknowledge smaller personal achievements too. It could be something as simple as successfully managing a month's budget without any disagreements or deciding to adopt a pet together. These important milestones, often overlooked, form the foundation of a meaningful connection.

- **Stroll Down Memory Lane:** Create a scrapbook or digital slideshow showcasing your journey together. Include movie tickets from films you've watched, photos from trips taken, or even screenshots of your text conversations.

- **Meaningful Gifts:** Instead of expensive presents, consider something with sentimental value. A handwritten letter expressing your feelings, a playlist featuring songs that define your relationship, or even a book that you believe your partner would adore.

- **Reflection is Key:** Celebrations should go beyond joy and gratitude; they should also provide an opportunity for reflection. Take the time to discuss what you have learned about each other, how you have grown as individuals and as a couple, and what aspirations you hold for the future. This process of reflection ensures that your relationship continues to evolve and progress.

- **Embracing Rituals:** Adding rituals to your celebrations adds an extra layer of significance. It can be as simple as watching the sunrise on your anniversary or planting a tree whenever you achieve a goal together. Over time, these traditions become part of the story of your relationship.

- **Engage Your Community:** While a relationship exists between two people, it is also part of a community that includes friends and family. Involve them in your celebrations! Their perspectives and shared memories can deepen your understanding and appreciation of milestones.

Embrace personal progress. It's important to celebrate not only the past but also look towards the future. Set goals together to nurture your relationship and achieve shared objectives. This mindset ensures that your bond remains vibrant and focused on reaching milestones.

Celebrating milestones and achievements goes beyond marking dates on a calendar. Recognizing and appreciating the journey of a relationship is crucial for fostering growth and establishing a foundation. It allows couples to build a future filled with shared dreams and aspirations. By giving importance to these moments, couples can ensure that their connection remains resilient, continuously evolving, and brimming with love.

Tips for Keeping the Spark Alive

Maintaining enthusiasm and passion in a long-term relationship can be challenging as time goes by. The initial excitement of falling in love may fade, making way for routine and familiarity. However, by investing effort into their relationship, couples can keep the flame of love burning brightly throughout their journey. Here are some practical suggestions to maintain romance:

- **Make Date Nights a Priority:** Remember those days when you both eagerly looked forward to your dates? Let's revive that tradition! Whether you're enjoying a dinner at home or having a fun movie night, regular date nights can reignite the spark between you and your partner.
- **Keep Things Spontaneous:** Avoid falling into a monotonous routine by surprising each other from time to time. These surprises don't have to be grand gestures; even leaving sweet notes or preparing breakfast for your partner can make all the difference.
- **Grow Together:** Consider exploring new experiences as a couple by enrolling in classes or workshops. Whether it's trying out dance lessons, pottery classes, or embarking on a language learning journey, acquiring skills as a team can strengthen your bond.
- **Foster Honest Communication:** It is crucial to have conversations with your partner about your desires, fantasies, and needs. By discussing

these aspects with each other, you create an atmosphere of trust and understanding that deepens your connection.

- **Embrace Physical Intimacy:** Remember that physical closeness goes beyond sex—it includes powerful gestures that promote affection and closeness in your relationship. Holding hands, giving hugs, or simply cuddling on the couch can foster a strong sense of connection. Make sure to set dedicated time for these meaningful acts of togetherness.

- **Embark on Exciting Adventures:** Exploring new places and going on thrilling adventures together can bring fresh perspectives to your relationship.

- **Take a Walk Down Memory Lane:** Spend some time reminiscing about the early days of your relationship. Look at photos, revisit meaningful places, and talk about those special moments when you first started dating. It's a way to cherish the journey you've taken together and reignite the reasons why you fell in love.

- **Set Goals as a Team:** Having shared objectives, such as saving for your dream home, planning a trip, or working towards fitness goals, can bring you closer as a couple. It gives you something to look forward to and allows both partners to work together harmoniously towards achieving those goals.

- **Be an Active Listener:** In our lives, we often hear but don't truly listen. Make an effort to practice listening when your partner speaks by giving them your undivided attention without any distractions. This shows that their thoughts and feelings are important to you and demonstrates interest in what they have to say.

- **Explore New Experiences Intimately:** Intimacy can also benefit from trying new things together in the bedroom! Let's talk openly about what we both desire and make sure that we're comfortable exploring activities that can enhance our intimacy together.

- **Express Gratitude and Give Compliments:** Don't underestimate the power of expressing gratitude and giving compliments. It's important to show appreciation to your partner as it reinforces how much you value your relationship.

- **Creating Rituals Together:** Whether it's enjoying a cup of coffee in the morning, taking walks together, or cooking meals as a team once a week, these shared moments become special and meaningful.

- **Connect Without Technology:** It's crucial to set aside dedicated times without technology. This means avoiding screens during meals or before bedtime to allow for moments of interaction and connection.

Three Hidden Techniques to Reignite Passion in Half a Minute

1. **The "Locked Eyes" Experiment:** In our fast-paced lives, we often overlook the importance of genuine, uninterrupted connection. Here's a simple yet profound tip: Try the "Locked Eyes" Experiment.

Instructions:

- Find a moment to share with your partner, perhaps during breakfast, after dinner, or any time you both are together.
- Create the atmosphere by eliminating distractions. Put away your phones, turn off the TV, and avoid playing any music. Instead, embrace the sounds around you.
- Now comes the challenge; sit face to face with your partner and simply gaze into each other's eyes. No talking, no physical contact. Just pure observation. Try to maintain eye contact for at least a minute.

Why is this exercise so effective?

- **Deep Connection:** Our eyes are considered windows to our souls. Looking into each other's eyes can convey emotions that words often struggle to express.
- **Vulnerability:** Sustaining eye contact without relying on verbal communication reveals an extraordinary level of vulnerability, creating a moment that can reignite feelings of intimacy.
- **Anticipation:** As time passes, you may feel an urge to smile, laugh, or even shed a tear, experiencing a rollercoaster of emotions within just 60 seconds.
- **Rediscovery:** You'll start noticing details about each other that often go unnoticed in daily life, like the shade of their eyes, a hidden freckle, or the way their eyes light up in a particular manner.

The "Locked Eyes" Challenge goes beyond a staring contest. It takes you on a journey of rediscovery and stands as proof of the profound power of genuine human connection. It serves as a reminder that sometimes the simplest actions can evoke the most profound emotions.

2. **The Whispered Memory Game:** Combine intimacy with nostalgia in this technique. When you're together, lean in close and whisper a

cherished memory into your partner's ear. It could be anything: the first time you held hands, a funny incident from a date, or even lyrics from a song that reminds you of them. The twist? Make sure it's something you've never shared before or a forgotten detail.

Effects of this unexpected revelation:

- **Surprise Factor:** Sharing a memory unexpectedly can instantly evoke a rush of emotions, bridging any emotional gaps between you.
- **Intimacy:** Whispering creates an intimate bubble, even amidst bustling surroundings. In that moment, it feels like it's just the two of you, connected by a shared past.
- **Nostalgia:** Reminiscing about shared moments can reignite the warmth and affection from earlier times.
- **Encourages Mutual Sharing:** Often, this game prompts your partner to share their memories in return, turning it into a beautiful exchange.

Relationships often hinge on these moments that leave the deepest impressions. The "Whispered Memory Game" is proof of that. It demonstrates how sometimes it takes just one minute and a whispered secret from the past to rekindle the present.

3. **The "Whispered Dreams" Technique:** Amidst our lives, we often overlook the profound impact softly spoken words can have and the enchantment they bring instantly. The "Whispered Dreams" trick combines spontaneity, intimacy, and a touch of surprise.

Instructions:

- **Dreams in Writing:** Both partners jot down a dream or longing on a piece of paper. It could be as simple as "dancing under the stars" or as daring as "skydiving together." Fold these papers and store them in a small pouch or container.
- **Random Timer:** Set a timer on your phone or watch to go off at any moment throughout the day.
- **Putting the Trick into Action:** When the timer goes off, approach your partner silently, take their hand, lean in close, and whisper into their ear the dream or desire you wrote down earlier.

The beauty of this technique:

- **Element of Intrigue:** The unexpected timer combined with the hushed secret creates an air of mystery, breaking free from routines.
- **Intimacy:** Whispering to each other creates an intimate moment, even in a crowded place.
- **Future Adventures:** These whispered dreams plant seeds for future adventures you can embark on as a couple.
- **Reigniting Curiosity:** Over time, both partners eagerly anticipate the whispered dream, reigniting a spark of curiosity and excitement in the relationship.

The "Whispered Dreams" hack is more than just a technique; it represents a promise of shared dreams and exciting adventures. It serves as a reminder that every day holds the potential for magic, and sometimes all it takes is a whisper to unlock it.

In the journey of love, remember that relationships require effort, attention, and nurturing—like any other aspect of life. By incorporating these tips and tricks into your routine, you can ensure that the spark remains alive and keeps your relationship vibrant, passionate, and fulfilling.

Overcoming Discrimination and Bias

Whatever your beliefs or sexual proclivities, in our society that strives for acceptance and inclusivity, queer couples still face various challenges. Dealing with discrimination and bias, whether they are subtle or obvious, can take a toll. However, love, resilience, and strategic approaches can help navigate these situations.

Educating for Advocacy You're not obligated to educate everyone you come across. However, dispelling misconceptions can be a powerful tool against ignorance. It's helpful to have a collection of resources, such as articles or documentaries that have personally impacted you. When faced with someone who's curious but misinformed, sharing these materials can turn potentially negative interactions into enlightening ones.

Building a Supportive Network Surround yourself with allies – friends and family who not only support your relationship but also stand up against discrimination. They can serve as your support system, intervening in challenging situations when necessary and providing backing afterwards.

Creating this network isn't about isolating yourself; it's about safeguarding your well-being while fostering respect.

Embracing Affirming Practices When navigating the difficulties of the world becomes overwhelming, turn inward and engage in activities that affirm your love and identity. You can celebrate your love story by attending LGBTQ+ events, joining support groups, or simply having a date night at a queer-friendly place. Remember that your love is beautiful and valid.

Setting Boundaries is Crucial It's important to recognize when it's worth engaging in a discussion and when it's best to walk away. Not every argument is worth fighting, as some people may hold views that cannot be changed, no matter how much you argue. Identify these situations and prioritize your mental well-being by establishing clear boundaries. It's perfectly acceptable to decline invitations or distance yourself from negative influences.

Taking Breaks from the World Choose whom you follow and interact with online, making sure they uplift and inform you. Don't hesitate to block or mute individuals who bring negativity into your digital space. Remember, taking care of your well-being is just as important as looking after your emotional health.

Seeking Guidance Through Therapy There's no shame in seeking guidance through therapy or counseling when needed. Professionals specializing in LGBTQ+ matters can provide coping strategies tailored to your experiences. They provide a space where you can openly discuss and process your emotions, which can be extremely valuable.

Celebrate the Victories Each time you stand up against prejudice or choose love over fear, it's worth acknowledging—even if it may seem small. These moments showcase your resilience and the deep affection between you and your partner.

Remember Your Self-Worth Your value is not determined by others' opinions. Your relationship, like any other, has its own unique beauty and challenges. Embrace the love, joy, and even the difficulties that shape your journey together.

In the face of adversities, the love that exists between couples shines brighter than ever. It serves as a testament to their strength, resilience, and the unwavering power of love that refuses to be constrained. Despite obstacles, with effective strategies and an unyielding spirit, queer couples can not only overcome external discrimination and prejudice but also thrive amidst them.

Creating Personalized Affirmations While there are many affirmations available, those that have the greatest impact are ones that truly resonate with your specific journey. Reflect on the strengths of your relationship, the obstacles you have triumphed over, and the love that binds you together. Use these reflections as a foundation to craft affirmations that genuinely speak to your heart.

For instance, "The love we share is genuine and awe-inspiring. Together we have the strength to overcome any challenge."

Incorporating Positive Affirmations into Everyday Life

To ensure that affirmations have an impact, it is essential to consistently practice them. Here are some ways you can effortlessly integrate them into your routine:

- **Morning Rituals:** Begin your day by reciting affirmations together. This simple act sets a tone for the day ahead and reinforces the deep connection you both share.
- **Visual Reminders:** Write down affirmations on notes and strategically place them around your home, especially in areas you visit frequently, like the bathroom mirror or refrigerator door. These visual cues serve as reminders of the strength and love that bind you together.
- **Journaling:** Take a few minutes each day to write down your affirmations in a journal. This practice allows for reflection on how your mindset has evolved over time, becoming more positive.

Embrace these suggestions and witness how personalized affirmations become a part of your daily life, nurturing an even stronger bond with yourself and your partner.

Utilize the reminder feature on your phones to set up alerts for your chosen affirmations. In today's fast-paced world, this method ensures that you never forget your affirmations, no matter how busy you are.

The Importance of Safe Spaces

Safe spaces are havens where individuals can express themselves freely without the fear of being judged, discriminated against, or harmed. For couples, specifically, these spaces serve as sanctuaries where their love is cherished, their identities are respected, and their experiences are validated.

Physical Safe Spaces: These can include LGBTQ+ community centers, welcoming cafes catering to individuals, or even the home of a trusted friend. Such places provide an inviting atmosphere where LGBTQ+ couples can truly be themselves, share their stories, and connect with others who understand their journey.

Digital Safe Spaces: Online platforms, forums, and social media groups designed specifically for the community can also serve as sanctuaries for those who may not have access to physical safe spaces. These platforms offer an avenue to share experiences, seek guidance, and find support from a like-minded community.

Creating Your Sanctuary: While community spaces are important for couples' well-being and sense of belonging, it is equally important for them to establish a safe haven within their own homes – a space where they can retreat from the outside world's pressures and celebrate their love in peace.

Personalize Your Environment: Infuse your home with symbols of love and acceptance, such as artwork and mementos that honor queer relationships. Make it uniquely yours—a reflection of your journey. Decorate your space with an array of colors or showcase photographs and artwork crafted by queer artists to reflect your individual identity. Emphasize the importance of dialogue within your home, creating an environment that encourages honest and authentic conversations. Engage in discussions with your partner, sharing experiences, fears, and aspirations to foster trust and understanding along the journey. Additionally, take the time to acknowledge and honor the beauty of love.

Every relationship deserves to be celebrated. This holds true for queer relationships as well. These relationships come with their unique set of challenges and victories.

Acknowledging Special Occasions: Take part in Pride parades, commemorate National Coming Out Day, or mark significant dates that hold personal meaning for your journey together. These celebrations are not just about the LGBTQ+ community at large; they symbolize the shared experiences of your queer partnership.

Commending Personal Milestones: Celebrate the day you first met, your first date, or the moment you both opened up about your identities. These personal milestones reflect your journey, showcasing the hurdles you've overcome and the love you've nurtured.

Establishing Your Traditions: Whether it's a monthly date night, an annual getaway, or even a special routine unique to your relationship, create traditions that are meaningful to both of you. These rituals serve as threads weaving the fabric of your shared life.

The Strength of Community: While it's crucial to celebrate your love as a couple, there is power in fostering connections within the LGBTQ+ community. Engage with organizations, attend events, workshops, or support groups. Not only do these avenues provide a sense of belonging but also offer opportunities for personal growth and advocacy for queer rights.

By embracing love openly and unapologetically, we contribute to a revolution in itself. In a world that often marginalizes or stigmatizes queer relationships, it is important to embrace your truth, create spaces that honor your love, and celebrate every aspect of your journey. This not only defies societal norms but also showcases the enduring power of love. Remember, every love story is beautiful in its unique way, with its own set of challenges, joys, and milestones. Treasure it, rejoice in it. Let it shine brightly in a world that craves more love.

The Experience of Coming Out in a Relationship; Navigating the Emotional Terrain

Coming out is a personal and transformative journey. When you are in a relationship, this process can be both thrilling and challenging since it involves not only yourself but also your partner. The emotional landscape of coming out within a relationship is complex and can encompass moments of exhilaration as well as uncertainty or clarity. Here's a step-by-step guide to navigating this terrain:

1. **Prioritize Self-Acceptance:** Before opening up to your partner about your truth, it's crucial to accept yourself first. Embracing your identity

forms the basis for communication with your partner. Take time for self-reflection, self-understanding, and self-acceptance. This self-awareness will serve as your guide as you move forward with the steps.

2. **Pick the Right Moment:** Timing is crucial. Find a moment when both you and your partner can have an uninterrupted conversation. This discussion needs time, focus, and a safe environment where both of you feel at ease.

3. **Start with Honesty:** Begin the conversation by being open and transparent. Share your emotions, fears, and hopes honestly. Let your partner understand why you're sharing this with them and how much their understanding and support mean to you. Remember, showing vulnerability is a sign of strength, and revealing your self is an incredibly courageous act.

4. **Be Prepared for Reactions:** Everyone processes information in their own way. Your partner might react with surprise, confusion, support, or even distance initially. Understand that they may need time to process things just like you did. Be patient and give them the space they require.

5. **Provide Resources:** Sometimes initial reactions stem from a lack of understanding. Offer books, articles, or documentaries that have been helpful to you during your journey of self-acceptance. These resources can bring clarity and facilitate better comprehension of what you're experiencing.

6. **Maintain Dialogue:** One conversation often isn't enough. It's important to keep communication open between you and your partner. Make sure to discuss your feelings, address any concerns, and be available to answer any questions they may have. This ongoing dialogue will help strengthen your connection and ensure that both of you are on the same page.

If necessary, don't hesitate to seek support like counseling or joining support groups. These resources can offer guidance, provide a space for discussions, and be incredibly helpful in navigating the complexities of coming out within a relationship.

Remember to celebrate your truth throughout this process. Coming out is not just about facing challenges; it's also a celebration of embracing your authentic self. Cherish the openness in your relationship and recognize the courage it took for you to share your truth. Appreciate the love and understanding from your partner as both of you navigate this journey together.

Understand that coming out is a process; it's not something that happens only once. As your relationship evolves and you encounter people or situations, there may be instances where you'll need to address your identity again. Approach each situation with honesty and understanding, just as you did before.

Lastly, continue nurturing your relationship beyond coming out. Remember that it's a shared journey between both of you. While coming out is a milestone, it's crucial to keep investing in the bond you share with love, care, and support. Engage in activities that you both enjoy, openly communicate, and make sure your relationship remains a space where both of you can be your true selves. The process of coming out in a relationship is profound, filled with moments of self-reflection, bravery, and deep connection. By navigating the journey with understanding, patience, and love, you lay the foundation for a relationship based on trust, authenticity, and an unbreakable bond. Remember that each step you take showcases your resilience and the love shared between you and your partner. Embrace it, cherish it, and let it guide you towards a future filled with empathy and acceptance.

PART IV; EMBRACING THE JOURNEY

Personal Growth in Relationships: Finding the Balance between Independence and Togetherness

Relationships in all their forms are like a beautiful tapestry woven together with shared experiences, emotions, and personal growth. However, within this shared journey lies an equilibrium between individuality and togetherness. It is crucial to embrace both aspects for a relationship to flourish, ensuring that each partner feels fulfilled as an individual while also being part of a couple.

The Importance of Individuality

Every person brings their unique set of experiences, dreams, and aspirations into a relationship. These personal characteristics define who we are and should never be overshadowed by the relationship itself. Instead, they should be nurtured.

1. **Creating Space for Self-Reflection:**
   - Taking time for oneself should not be seen as distancing from the relationship but rather as an opportunity for self-reflection. It allows us to gain self-understanding and brings perspectives back into the partnership. Whether it's engaging in solo hobbies or activities like meditation or simply spending time absorbed in reading or contemplation—these moments of solitude can prove rejuvenating.

2. **Pursuing Personal Goals:**
   - While shared goals are undoubtedly important in any relationship, it is equally vital to maintain one's aspirations alongside them. Whether it's advancing in a career, acquiring skills, or pursuing a passion project, these personal pursuits greatly influence and shape identity.

3. **Cultivate Groups of Friends:**
   - While having mutual friends is amazing, maintaining separate social circles provides an opportunity for diverse experiences. It brings perspectives and stories to the table, making conversations more enriching.

The Beauty of Being Together

While individual growth is crucial, the essence of a relationship lies in shared experiences. It revolves around creating memories, understanding each other's ups and downs, and evolving as a unit.

1. **Building Shared Moments:**
   - From embarking on adventures to exploring new cuisines or simply indulging in binge-watching sessions, shared experiences forge lasting memories. They become stories that couples fondly recall, strengthening their bond.
2. **Open Channels of Communication:**
   - Engaging in discussions about personal goals and aspirations ensures that both partners are aligned. This fosters understanding and prevents growth from causing emotional distance.
3. **Supporting Each Other's Aspirations:**
   - While pursuing dreams, having the support of one's partner can be empowering. Celebrating each other's accomplishments, being there during setbacks, and consistently encouraging one another to aim higher are vital components of this dynamic.

Activities for Balancing Individuality and Togetherness

In the dance of relationships, maintaining equilibrium between individuality and unity can be both challenging yet necessary. Recognizing and appreciating each partner's identity while nurturing the shared bond that connects you is essential.

Here are some inclusive activities that cater to relationships, ensuring that every couple, regardless of their background or identity, can find ways to honor both their uniqueness and their journey together.

1. **Creating Personal Vision Boards:**
   - Begin by making vision boards where each partner uses images, quotes, and symbols that reflect their personal dreams, aspirations, and values. Then share these boards with each other. This activity allows partners to express their individuality while also fostering understanding and support for each other's dreams.
2. **Building a Shared Bucket List:**
   - While individual goals are important, it's equally crucial to have shared dreams. Make a bucket list together consisting of experiences you both want to have as a couple. It could involve

traveling to destinations, attending special events, or even trying out new hobbies as a team. This list serves as a testament to the shared journey you envision together.

3. **Taking Solo Day Outings:**
   - Set aside a day where each partner spends time doing activities they enjoy the most. Whether it's exploring a museum, taking a nature walk, or participating in workshops or classes of interest. This dedicated time allows for space and experiences within the relationship. On reconvening, share your respective experiences with one another.

4. **Joint Journaling:**
   - Keep a shared journal where both partners can write about their emotions, experiences, and aspirations. This practice promotes communication and helps partners gain a better understanding of each other's perspectives, bridging the gap between individuality and togetherness.

5. **DIY Project:**
   - Engage in a do-it-yourself project. It could involve building something for your shared space or creating a piece of artwork together. This process highlights teamwork and the beauty of co-creating something symbolizing unity.

6. **Attend Workshops:**
   - Take part in workshops that focus on self-awareness and personal growth. Then share what you've learned and your experiences with each other. This activity encourages development while also emphasizing the value of bringing new insights back into the relationship.

7. **Date Night with a Twist:**
   - Plan a date night where each partner chooses an activity without revealing it to the other beforehand. This element of surprise allows partners to introduce each other to their interests, blending individuality with shared experiences.

8. **Mutual Support System:**
   - Set time to discuss individual goals and how you can support each other in achieving them. This practice strengthens the bond by highlighting support and understanding.

9. **Craft a Playlist for Your Relationship:**

- Both partners can contribute songs that resonate with their emotions, memories, and shared experiences. This playlist becomes a blend of preferences and cherished moments symbolizing the perfect harmony between personal uniqueness and togetherness.

10. **Take Time to Reflect and Realign:**
- Set aside moments to sit together and reflect on how you both have been maintaining a healthy balance between independence and unity. Openly discuss what's working well and what might need readjustment. This activity ensures that your relationship remains a space where both individuality and togetherness are embraced and nurtured.

In the journey of relationships, it's crucial to remember that while being unified is wonderful, it's the colors of each individual that make the overall picture vivid. By engaging in activities that honor both identity and the shared connection, couples can ensure that their relationship thrives as a beautiful blend of independence and togetherness.

Seeking Assistance

In any relationship, there are challenges. While many couples navigate these obstacles with resilience, there are times when seeking assistance becomes not just beneficial but necessary. However, societal stigmas and misconceptions often cloud the decision to seek therapy. Overcoming these stigmas is crucial as it allows couples to access the support they truly deserve.

Therapy has long been viewed skeptically in cultures and societies. Some mistakenly perceive it as a sign of weakness, assuming that strong individuals or couples should be able to resolve their issues on their own. Others worry about being judged or becoming subjects of gossip if they admit to seeking therapy. Moreover, there is a misconception that therapy is only for those on the brink of breaking up or dealing with severe problems.

Let's debunk some of these myths and misconceptions:

1. **Therapy as an Indicator of Weakness:**
- Recognizing the importance of support and taking proactive measures to seek help demonstrates strength and self-awareness. It shows a commitment to growing and is not an admission of defeat.

2. **Fear of Being Judged:**

- Prioritizing the well-being of a relationship over others' opinions is a testament to the dedication between partners. Every relationship encounters challenges, and there is no shame in seeking assistance to navigate through them.

3. **Therapy is Not Just for Crisis:**
   - Therapy can be beneficial at any stage of a relationship. It provides tools, strategies, and insights that enable couples to better understand each other, communicate effectively, and overcome challenges more smoothly.

4. **Concerns About Impartiality:**
   - Reputable therapists strive for impartiality. Their goal is to create an environment where both partners feel genuinely heard and understood without any judgment.

When embarking on a journey of love and commitment, there should be no shame in seeking guidance or support through therapy—a resource that helps couples navigate the complexities of being together. By acknowledging and addressing biases while embracing the advantages of therapy, couples have the opportunity to delve into a level of comprehension, enhance their communication abilities, and foster a stronger bond.

Getting Ready for Professional Guidance
Choosing to seek guidance for relationship challenges demonstrates commendable dedication to personal growth, understanding, and nurturing the connection you share with your partner. However, deciding to pursue therapy or counseling is just the initial step. Proper preparation plays a role in maximizing the benefits and ensuring that both partners are on the same page.

Recognizing the Need: Before starting therapy, it's crucial to understand why you are seeking assistance. Are you looking to resolve conflicts, improve communication, rebuild trust, or strengthen an already solid bond? Identifying these reasons can bring clarity and direction to your sessions.

Choosing the Right Therapist: Not all therapists are alike. Some specialize in particular methodologies, while others have expertise in dealing with specific relationship challenges. It's important to research therapists, consider their areas of specialization, and read reviews or testimonials. It may also be beneficial to have a session or consultation to determine if their approach aligns with your needs.

Setting Expectations: Understand that therapy is not a solution that will instantly solve all problems. It is a process that often requires time, effort, and patience. Establishing realistic expectations with your partner can help avoid potential letdowns and ensure full dedication to the process.

Openness and Vulnerability: Being open and vulnerable is a key element in effective therapy. It involves being willing to share your feelings, concerns, fears, and hopes honestly. Being prepared to be vulnerable and attentive can make therapy sessions more productive.

Committing to Action: Therapy often includes homework—activities, exercises, or practices to work on between sessions. These tasks are intended to reinforce what you've learned. Being prepared to dedicate yourself to these actions and diligently practice them can significantly enhance the benefits you gain from therapy.

Financial Considerations: Discuss budgets, understand insurance coverage options, or explore sliding scale payment arrangements to prevent stress. It's also crucial for both partners involved in therapy to allocate time for sessions and any recommended exercises or practices.

Reflection and Feedback: Taking time for reflection after a few sessions is valuable. Ask yourself if you feel heard and understood by your therapist? Are the sessions providing value? Do you feel aligned with the approach being taken? Providing feedback and being adaptable can guide future sessions towards greater effectiveness.

Building a Support Network: While the therapist provides expert guidance, having support outside of therapy can be incredibly valuable. Friends, family members, or support groups can offer perspectives, lend an ear, or simply be there as a source of support.

Privacy: Ensure that your chosen professional follows confidentiality protocols. Feeling safe and secure in knowing that your conversations remain private is essential.

Embracing the Journey: Therapy is a journey characterized by ups and downs. Being prepared for this roller coaster ride and understanding that it's all part of the process can make the journey smoother.

Recommended Resources: Therapy Platforms and Websites Navigating the complexities of relationships requires understanding, patience, and often guidance. Here is a list of inclusive platforms and websites catering to diverse relationship dynamics:

1. **BetterHelp:** An esteemed online therapy platform that connects individuals and couples with licensed therapists.
2. **Pride Counseling:** Tailored specifically for the LGBTQ+ community, offering online counseling services.
3. **Talkspace:** An online therapy platform that provides guidance for individuals, couples, and even adolescents.
4. **The Gottman Institute Blog:** Renowned for its insights into relationships, offering articles and advice for both heterosexual and LGBTQ+ dynamics.
5. **PsychCentral:** Offering articles, therapist directories, and reviews on various mental health apps.
6. **TherapyRoute:** A comprehensive directory to help find therapists based on criteria.
7. **LGBTQ+ Couples Institute:** Focused on LGBTQ+ couples, offering resources, workshops, and training.
8. **The Couples Center:** Provides resources for all couples, including sections for diverse relationship dynamics.
9. **Relationship Alive Podcast:** Discusses relationships in general, often featuring episodes exploring various types of relationships.

When it comes to love and relationships it's crucial for everyone regardless of the type of relationship, they have to find the support and resources they need. The digital world provides platforms and websites that prioritize inclusivity and understanding. As you embark on your journey in a relationship these resources can serve as a guide to help you navigate challenges and foster deeper connection and understanding.

Final Thoughts: Embracing the Journey, Celebrating Progress and Facing Future Challenges

Relationships, much like life itself, are a journey filled with dynamics that evolve, change, and sometimes encounter difficulties. As we conclude this guide, it's vital to recognize that what truly defines a relationship is the progress made and the challenges overcome.

Acknowledging Progress Each step taken in a relationship signifies the commitment and love shared between partners. It's important to take moments to reflect on how far you've come. This could be successfully navigating financial planning, improving communication, implementing techniques like EFT or the Gottman Method, or simply learning to cherish small moments of joy and connection more deeply. Celebrating these achievements is crucial, whether through grand gestures or simple acts of appreciation and reflective conversations.

Facing Future Challenges While celebrating progress is important, we must also be prepared for future challenges. No relationship is immune to ups and downs, but the approach to these challenges matters. Embracing them as opportunities for growth can strengthen the bond between partners, teaching resilience, understanding, and patience.

There may be various challenges ahead, both external factors like societal changes or personal crises, and internal factors arising from evolving desires or relationship dynamics. However, equipped with the knowledge and strategies provided in this guide, you are better prepared to confront these challenges.

Remember, a successful relationship isn't defined by the absence of obstacles but by the ability to navigate them together, drawing strength from one another and the love you share.

Carrying Lessons Forward As you move forward, carry with you the lessons learned, cherished moments experienced, and love nurtured. Let them illuminate your path ahead. Shared experiences—both joyful and difficult—create a tapestry of memories, emotions, and love.

In the words of Leo Tolstoy, "What truly matters in creating a marriage is not so much compatibility but rather how you handle incompatibility." Celebrate progress and embrace challenges as part of your journey. Cherish the love and connection that binds you together.

Here's to a future filled with understanding, growth, and boundless love. Wishing you a safe and beautiful journey as you continue this adventure together.

Tips and Tricks: Ensuring Progress in Relationships

Embarking on the journey of love and partnership is rewarding, yet it requires effort, understanding, and a commitment to personal growth. To nurture and continuously develop your relationship, consider these tips and strategies:

1. **The "Memory Jar" Method**: Create a jar to capture special moments. Jot down significant experiences, from impromptu dances to deep conversations, and place them in the jar. Revisit these cherished memories during challenging times or at the end of the year to remember the bond you share.

2. **Monthly "Growth Dates"**: Dedicate one date each month to discuss your progress as a couple. Reflect on what you've learned, areas of growth, and aspects that need focus in the coming month. This proactive approach ensures alignment and prioritizes growth.

3. **The "Skill Swap"**: Dedicate a day to teach each other something new. This is a great way to bond, learn, and appreciate each other's talents and interests.

4. **"Future Letter" Writing**: Write letters to your future selves discussing hopes, dreams, and relationship goals. Seal them and set a date in the future to open and read them together. This can help you see how aspirations have evolved and which ones you've accomplished.

5. **The "Unplugged Evening" Rule**: Designate one evening a week to put aside all digital devices. Use this time to connect, play board games, or simply talk. The depth of connection experienced without distractions can be profound.

6. **"Adventure Challenges"**: Challenge each other to try something new every month. Whether exploring a hobby, visiting new places, or attending workshops, these activities can strengthen your bond and add excitement to your relationship.

7. **Lifelong Learning**: Invest in your relationship by attending workshops, reading books, or taking courses together. There's always something new to discover and implement.

8. **"Moments of Appreciation"**: Set reminders on your phone for "Appreciation Time". When they pop up, take a moment to express

something you value about your partner. These instances of gratitude can significantly enhance positivity in your relationship.

9. **Craft a "Relationship Vision Board"**: Create a vision board specifically for your relationship. Fill it with images, quotes, and mementos symbolizing your shared goals and aspirations.

Remember, love and partnership are about growth and evolution. By incorporating these strategies, you not only ensure that the relationship remains vibrant but also that it continually adapts to life's changes. Small efforts come together to create a beautiful and fulfilling relationship.

Thank you for allowing this guide to be part of your journey towards connection and enduring love. The path ahead is illuminated by the love you've nurtured and the wisdom you've acquired. Here's to your future—a future where your love story flourishes, where open communication flows effortlessly, and where your bond serves as a testament to lasting love.

Dear Reader

I genuinely hope that this book has offered you insights and advice on how to cultivate a relationship.

As an independent author your input is incredibly valuable to me.

Your opinion holds importance so I kindly request you to consider writing an honest review. By following this link, it will directly take you to the Amazon reviewing page:

https://www.amazon.com/review/create-review/?asin=**BOCJSYZW57**

Will only take around 30 seconds of your time.

Thank you sincerely for your support.

Warmest regards,

Esther Collins

GET YOUR EXCLUSIVE BONUS HERE!

SCAN THE QR CODE OR COPY AND PASTE THE URL

https://drive.google.com/drive/folders/1zqFpPwtlwkzx9LGfFEPFMfbTnJKe6oTV?usp=sharing